"I'm coming to you as a woman"

By Jasmin Miles

Copyright © 2025 by Jasmin Miles
All rights reserved. No part of this book may be reproduced in any form without permission from the author or publisher, except as permitted by U.S. copyright law. To request permission, contact Jasministries3130@gmail.com

I'm Coming to You as a Woman

Hey friend, before we turn the first page, I need you to know something, this isn't just a book of stories. This is a conversation. A heart-to-heart. A safe kitchen table with warm tea, a box of tissues, and no judgment.

I'm coming to you as a woman.

Not as someone who has it all figured out. Not as someone who's never made mistakes. I'm coming to you as someone who's walked through valleys, stumbled over my own feet, wrestled with God, and still found His hand reaching for me. I'm coming as a sister, as a friend, who knows that womanhood is both beautiful and brutal, full of high praise and heavy burdens, holy moments and hard nights.

When I say, *"I'm coming to you as a woman,"* I'm not just echoing the voices of the past, I'm stepping into our present.

Because being a woman today is still complex. We live in a world that applauds independence but often ignores loneliness. A society that praises beauty but overlooks the soul. A culture that demands we "do it all" climb the ladder, raise the family, heal the wounds, fight the battles and still smile while we do it.

To come to you as a woman at this moment is to come with honesty. To admit that sometimes we're tired. Sometimes we feel unseen. Sometimes we compare, we compete, we collapse under the weight of expectations.

But it also means to come with strength. Because being a woman today is also about resilience. It's about building when resources are low, loving when hearts are heavy, showing up when it would be easier to quit. It's about carrying generations in our prayers while carrying groceries in our arms.

Coming to you as a woman in today's society means I'm not hiding behind a mask. I'm showing up real, raw, and redeemed. It means I stand shoulder-to-shoulder with you in every role; daughter, sister, mother, leader, friend. And together, we can remember that womanhood is not a burden to survive, but a calling to walk out with grace, courage, and God's power.

In these pages, you're going to hear from women whose names are written in the most important Book ever given, the Bible. Some you've known since Sunday School and Vacation Bible School. Some you might have skimmed over without realizing they had something to say to you. But in this book, they speak in their own voices. First-person. Raw. Real. And as they tell their stories, you'll notice something, they're not speaking from history, they're speaking into your right now.

Eve will take you back to the garden and whisper about choices. Sarah will sit beside you and tell you what waiting really feels like. Hagar will look you in the eyes and remind you that God sees you even in the desert. Deborah will rally your courage. Ruth will invite you into covenant loyalty. And the women of the New Testament; Mary, Elizabeth, Martha, the Samaritan Woman, Mary Magdalene; will show you how an encounter with Jesus changes everything.

Some of these women will inspire you to rise. Others will warn you to turn. But every single one of them will meet you where you are and call you closer to the heart of God.

This book is not a museum tour through biblical history. It's a meeting place between your life and theirs. And if you lean in, you might just hear the Spirit saying through their voices, *"your story matters too."*

So take a breath. Let's walk together through these pages. Laugh a little. Cry if you need to. Be challenged. Be comforted. And above all, be reminded that you're not alone, you're part of a great cloud of witnesses, women who have lived and loved, fought and failed, prayed and persevered, and still made it through by the grace of God.

This is not just history; it is prophecy.

Every woman in these pages still speaks. Their voices echo across generations, whispering warnings, singing victories, and declaring promises. Through them, we learn that the choices of one life can ripple into eternity.

I'm coming to you as a woman.
And I'm inviting you to come as you are.

Table of Contents

Prologue

Women in God's Story: A Prophetic Journey

Part I – Beginnings & Patriarchs

1. Eve: *I'm Coming to You as the First Woman* (Genesis 2–3)

2. Naamah: *I'm Coming to You as a Woman Remembered in a World of Violence* (Genesis 4:22)

3. Sarah: *I'm Coming to You as a Woman Who Waited* (Genesis 12–23; Hebrews 11:11)

4. Hagar: *I'm Coming to You as a Woman Who Was Seen* (Genesis 16; 21:8–21)

5. Rebekah: *I'm Coming to You as a Woman of Influence* (Genesis 24; 27)

6. Leah: *I'm Coming to You as a Woman Who Learned to Praise* (Genesis 29–30)

7. Rachel: *I'm Coming to You as a Woman Who Waited and Wept* (Genesis 29–30; 35:16–20)

8. Tamar: I'm Coming to You as a Woman fighting for my place in promise (Genesis 38; Matthew 1:3)

Part II – Exodus & Wilderness

9. Shiphrah: *I'm Coming to You as a Woman Who Defied Pharaoh* (Exodus 1:15–21)

10. Puah: *I'm Coming to You as a Woman Who Protected Life* (Exodus 1:15–21)

11. Jochebed: *I'm Coming to You as a Mother Who Hid a Deliverer* (Exodus 2:1–10; Hebrews 11:23)

12. Miriam: *I'm Coming to You as a Woman Who Sang of Victory* (Exodus 2:4–8; 15:20–21; Numbers 12)

13. Zipporah: *I'm Coming to You as a Woman Who Stood in the Gap* (Exodus 2:21; 4:24–26)

Part III – The Judges Era

14. Deborah: *I'm Coming to You as a Woman Who Led Boldly* (Judges 4–5)

15. Jael: *I'm Coming to You as a Woman Who Finished the Fight* (Judges 4:17–22; 5:24–27)

Part IV – Conquest & Settlement

16. Rahab: *I'm Coming to You as a Woman Redeemed* (Joshua 2; 6:22–25; Matthew 1:5)

17. Delilah: *I'm Coming to You as a Woman Who Misused Her Power* (Judges 16:4–22)

18. Hannah: *I'm coming to Your as a Woman who Prayed Through the Pain* (1 Samuel 1–2)

19. Peninnah: *I'm Coming to You as a Woman Who Provoked* (1 Samuel 1:2–7)

20. Orpah: *I'm Coming to You as a Woman Who Turned Back* (Ruth 1:4–14)

21. Ruth: *I'm Coming to You as a Woman Who Chose Covenant* (Ruth 1–4; Matthew 1:5)

22. Naomi: *I'm Coming to You as a Woman Who Returned* (Ruth 1–4)

Part V – Kings & Kingdoms

23. Abigail: *I'm Coming to You as a Woman of Wisdom* (1 Samuel 25)

24. Bathsheba: *I'm Coming to You as a Woman Restored* (2 Samuel 11–12; 1 Kings 1–2)

25. Tamar (Daughter of King David): *I'm Coming to You as a Woman Who Survived Violation* (2 Samuel 13:1–22)

26. Rizpah: *I'm Coming to You as a Woman Who Wouldn't Leave* (2 Samuel 21:8–14)

27. Jezebel: *I'm Coming to You as a Woman Who Chose the Wrong Throne* (1 Kings 16:31–33; 18–21; 2 Kings 9:30–37)

28. Huldah: *I'm Coming to You as a Woman Who Spoke God's Word* (2 Kings 22:14–20; 2 Chronicles 34:22–28)

29. Daughters of Job: *We're Coming to You as Women of Beauty After Ashes* (Job 42:13–15)

30. Isaiah's Wife: *I'm Coming to You as a Mother of a Sign* (Isaiah 8:3)

Part VI – Exile & Return

31. Esther: *I'm coming to you as a woman who had Courage in the Face of Fear* (Book of Esther)

32. Noadiah: *I'm Coming to You as a Woman Who Warns* (Nehemiah 6:14)

33. Proverbs 31 Woman: *I'm Coming to You as a Woman of Strength* (Proverbs 31:10–31)

Part VII – The Coming of Christ

34. Elizabeth: *I'm Coming to You as a Woman Who Carried Promise* (Luke 1:5–25, 39–45, 57–66)

35. Mary, Mother of Jesus: *I'm Coming to You as a Woman Who Said Yes* (Luke 1:26–38; 2; John 19:25–27)

36. Anna: *I'm Coming to You as a Woman Who Waited in Worship* (Luke 2:36–38)

Part VIII – Women in Jesus' Ministry

37. Samaritan Woman: *I'm Coming to You as a Woman Who Dropped Her Jar* (John 4:1–42)

38. Mary Magdalene: *I'm Coming to You as a Woman Delivered* (Luke 8:1–3; John 20:1–18)

39. Martha: *I'm Coming to You as a Woman Who Served* (Luke 10:38–42; John 11:1–44)

40. Mary of Bethany: *I'm Coming to You as a Woman Who Sat at His Feet* (Luke 10:38–42; John 11–12)

41. Joanna: *I'm Coming to You as a Woman Who Supported the Mission* (Luke 8:1–3; 24:10)

42. Woman with the Issue of Blood: *I'm Coming to You as a Woman Who Touched the Hem* (Mark 5:25–34; Luke 8:43–48)

Part IX – The Early Church

43. Dorcas (Tabitha): *I'm Coming to You as a Woman Who Clothed the Needy* (Acts 9:36–42)

44. Daughters of Philip: *We're Coming to You as Women Who Speak Truth* (Acts 21:8–9)

45. Phoebe: *I'm Coming to You as a Woman Trusted with the Word* (Romans 16:1–2)

46. Priscilla: *I'm Coming to You as a Woman Who Taught Truth* (Acts 18:1–3, 18–28; Romans 16:3–5)

47. Junia: *I'm Coming to You as a Woman Known Among the Apostles* (Romans 16:7)

Closing

48. Be Made Whole: *An invitation to step into healing, calling, and fullness in Christ.*

Epilogue

The Women Still Speak: A Prophetic Charge for Today

PART I

Patriarchs & Early Beginnings

The story of women begins in the garden and stretches into the birth of nations. From Eve's choice to Sarah's faith, these women set the foundation of humanity's story with God.

CHAPTER ONE

Eve ~ I'm Coming to You as the First Woman
How my choice in Eden still speaks to yours today (Genesis 2–3)

I'm coming to you as a woman who knows the weight of choice. Guard your ears before you lose your ground.

I'm Coming to You as the First Woman. Let me tell you where I went wrong. I was the first woman to walk in God's perfect garden, the first to hear His voice in the cool of the day, and the first to feel the ache of separation when sin entered the world. I had beauty without makeup, a home without rent, and peace without fear. Everything I needed was right there in the garden. But, even in paradise, the wrong voice can pull you out of God's will.

I still remember the day that serpent slid up on me. He didn't come hissing threats. No, he came with *questions.* I didn't just eat the fruit, I reached for something God hadn't given me yet.

You know what it's like, don't you? To see something that looks good, to hear a voice that twists truth just enough to make it sound reasonable, to take a step that can't be undone. For you, it may not be something as simple as eating a forbidden fruit, but it may be bad advice from the wrong friend, listening to social media lies or giving in to a charming man's words that steer you off of God's path.

The serpent didn't make me sin, it made me *think about it.* You know how we like to overthink and or stay in our head.

I should have walked away. I should have called on my husband. I should have shut that conversation down. But instead, I entertained it. And the longer I listened, the more the lies started sounding like freedom and God's truth started sounding like restriction.

I let curiosity outrun obedience. And friend, the cost was high. I told myself, *"It's just a bite, what's the harm?"*
But, it wasn't just about the fruit. It was about trust.

The moment I chose the serpent's word over God's word, I stepped outside of His covering.

The result? My husband and I lost our place in the garden. We lost peace, protection, and the closeness we had with God. I can still feel the ache of that loss.

But here's what I've learned: even in exile, God still covers His daughters. I thought it was over for me, that I'd be cast out with nothing. But even in judgment, God showed mercy. He made garments for Adam and I to cover our shame (Genesis 3:21).
That's the thing about God, even when we fall, He doesn't strip us bare; He covers us so we can begin again. He clothed me before sending me out. He gave me children. He let me still hear His voice. My failure wasn't the end of my story. And yours doesn't have to be either.

Guard your heart from the whispers that question God's goodness. Trust His "no" as much as His "yes." And remember, even if you've taken the wrong bite, His grace will still find you.

I'm telling you this because I don't want you to make my mistake. You will hear voices that sound wise, loving, or logical, but they will lead you away from what God already told you.
You don't owe every voice a seat at your table.

My Advice to You

Know His voice for yourself. Don't rely on hearsay; spend time in His presence so you can tell the difference. **Cut off the conversation early.** The enemy's bait always comes wrapped in something attractive. **Remember the cost.** Disobedience always costs more than you expect.

Hold On To This

"My sheep hear My voice, and I know them, and they follow Me." (John 10:27). *"Submit yourselves, then, to God. Resist the devil, and he will*

flee from you." (James 4:7). *"Many are the plans in a person's heart, but it is the Lord's purpose that prevails."* (Proverbs 19:21)

If I could go back, I'd guard my ears like my life depended on it, because it did.

Don't lose your ground over a conversation that never should have happened.

CHAPTER TWO

Naamah ~ I'm Coming to You as a Woman Remembered in a World of Violence

When darkness surrounds, your name can still carry light.
"...and the sister of Tubalcain was Naamah." Genesis 4:22

"I'm coming to you as a woman who lived in a world where sin was normal and had to decide what my life would stand for."

I'm coming to you as a woman whose name slipped into Scripture in the middle of a dark genealogy. My name isn't as famous as Eve's, but I was there in the days before the flood. My father, Lamech, was a man of vengeance. My brothers were inventors, one of tents and livestock, another of instruments, another of iron and bronze. We lived in a world quick to boast, quick to sin, quick to kill.

And then, there was me. Just a daughter. Just a sister. No mighty inventions. No recorded accomplishments. Only a name, Naamah. In Hebrew, it means pleasant, beautiful, sweet.

Sometimes your story won't look as grand as the people around you. Others may build cities, make music, forge tools, even wield violence to be remembered. But sometimes God includes you simply because your presence, your spirit, your quietness was a contrast to the chaos of your world.

I wasn't perfect, but in a family line bent on destruction, God let my name mean pleasant. That tells me He sees not just the warriors or kings, but the women who quietly carry His image in hostile places.

Friend, never think your life is too small to matter. Your name, your presence, your witness, even in a violent, broken culture is still seen. And sometimes, being light in the middle of darkness is the greatest legacy of all.

I'm Just Coming to You as a Woman

who knows what it's like to stand in a place where evil is popular and righteousness is rare.

It's not easy, but your life can be a quiet protest against the culture, a living testimony that God's ways are still good.

What I Want You to Know

Your surroundings don't have to define your story. God always notices those who remain faithful in dark times. And, one life can still shine in a corrupt generation.

So, Hold On To This

"But Noah found favor in the eyes of the Lord." (Genesis 6:8) ; If God saw Noah, He sees you. *"Do not be conformed to this world, but be transformed by the renewal of your mind."* (Romans 12:2). *"Arise, shine, for your light has come, and the glory of the Lord rises upon you."* (Isaiah 60:1)

I'm coming to you as a woman to tell you not to underestimate the power of living set apart. You may feel small, but in the eyes of God, you are a light in the darkness.

CHAPTER THREE

Sarah ~ I'm Coming to You as a Woman Who Waited
The journey of trusting God's promise against all odds. (Genesis 12–23; Hebrews 11:11)

"I'm coming to you as a woman to tell you not to rush what God promised you."

I'm Coming to You as a Woman who knows what it feels like to wait. I know what it's like to hear God speak a promise and then stare at the years as they pass by with no sign of it coming true. I was the wife of Abraham, and God Himself told us we would have a son. But I grew old watching my hope wrinkle alongside my skin. I know what it feels like to have a promise from God… and nothing to show for it. This doesn't have to be a child. It could be marriage, kids, a career or even ministry success. Year after year I waited for the child God said would come. And year after year, my womb stayed empty.

You have to understand, in my time, a woman's value was often tied to the children she could bear. And me? I had none. I was loved by my husband, yes, but I was still *ashamed*. And with each passing year, the promise started feeling like a joke. I laughed the first time I heard the prophecy, not out of joy, but disbelief. How could I, a barren woman, bear a child? And in my frustration, I tried to "help" God, giving my husband Hagar. But forcing His promise in my way only caused heartache.

One day, I thought I had the perfect solution. I told my husband, "Go sleep with my servant Hagar. Maybe I can build my family through her." I know, it sounds wild. But when you've been waiting and you can't see how God will do it, shortcuts start looking like wisdom. And so, Ishmael was born. But he wasn't the promised child. My "solution" brought more pain than blessing; jealousy, division, and a wedge between me and the very people I loved.

Here's the thing, my mistake didn't cancel God's promise.
When I was 90 years old (yes, ninety) God gave me Isaac. The child he had spoken about all those years before. And when I laughed at the

thought of it, God basically said, *"Is anything too hard for Me?"* (Genesis 18:14). Then, when it seemed too late, God showed me it's never too late for Him. Isaac's cry filled our tent, and my laughter turned from bitter to sweet. I learned something in that moment: God's timing is not about my calendar. His promise doesn't expire because of my age, my doubts, or my detours.

Friend, if God has spoken, time cannot cancel His word. Don't compromise to make His promise happen. Wait. Trust. He's faithful. And when the miracle comes, you'll laugh, the kind of laugh that wipes away every tear you cried in the waiting.

I'm coming to you as a woman,

who knows what it's like to wait and to get it wrong. When God promises you something, don't let impatience trick you into birthing something He never ordered. An Ishmael will always cost more than the wait for your Isaac.

My Advice to You

Don't confuse delay with denial. Just because it hasn't happened yet doesn't mean it won't. **Refuse to settle for a substitute.** If it's not what God said, it's not the promise. **Trust His timing.** Sometimes the wait is shaping you for the very thing you're asking for.

Hold On To This

"Is anything too hard for the Lord? At the appointed time I will return to you… and Sarah shall have a son." (Genesis 18:14). *"For the vision is yet for an appointed time… though it tarry, wait for it; because it will surely come."* (Habakkuk 2:3). *"Let us not grow weary in doing good, for at the proper time we will reap a harvest if we do not give up."* (Galatians 6:9

Take it from me, God's promise is worth the wait. Don't birth an Ishmael when He's preparing your Isaac.

CHAPTER FOUR

Hagar ~ I'm Coming to You as a Woman Who Was Seen
God found me in the wilderness, and He sees you too. (Genesis 16; 21:8–21)

"I'm coming to you as a woman who knows what it feels like to be used"

I'm Coming to You as a Woman who was seen and heard. "Even if they pushed you out, God hasn't forgotten you." I wasn't a wife; I was a servant. My life was lived at the mercy of others' decisions. When Sarah gave me to Abraham, I became pregnant, but I also became resented. Things got so bad, I ran into the desert. Alone. Afraid. Unwanted.

I didn't ask for this.
I didn't ask to be part of some woman's plan, Sarah's plan to be exact.
I was just a servant in her house. loyal, obedient, doing my work.

Then one day she told me, "Go sleep with my husband. Build my family for me."
I felt like I didn't have a choice. In my position, saying no wasn't an option. So I did what I was told.

When I became pregnant, everything changed.
I wasn't just a servant anymore, I was carrying the master's child.
And, I'm not going to lie… I started to get prideful. I looked at Sarah differently.
But her reaction was worse, she became harsh with me, and her jealousy burned like fire.

The tension got so bad, I ran.
Pregnant, alone, and with nowhere to go, I fled into the desert.
I thought I was running from her, but I was really running into God's plan.

It was there, in the wilderness, that I met Him, the God who sees me.
An angel of the Lord found me and called me by name.

Not "servant girl." Not "mistress' maid." Not "the problem." He called me **Hagar**.

And He told me to go back, to submit, but not without a promise. He said my son would be named Ishmael, which means "God hears," and that my descendants would be too many to count.

But that's where He found me, the Angel of the Lord, calling me by name. Me, a slave, seen by the God of Abraham. He gave me direction, He gave me a future, and He gave me a name for Him: El Roi, the God who sees me.

Friend, you may feel invisible, overlooked, or like your pain is a side note in someone else's story. But I promise you, there is a God who sees you. He knows where you've come from, and He knows where you're going. You are not lost to Him.

Do you know what it's like to be seen when you feel invisible? To have God find you when you've been pushed out? That day I gave Him a name: **El Roi**, "The God Who Sees Me" (Genesis 16:13). Because in a world where I was just a body to be used, He reminded me I was a soul to be loved.

What I Want You to Know

I know what it feels like to be discarded, undervalued, and unloved. I know what it feels like to be treated as disposable, feeling invisible at work, in relationships, or family.
But here's the truth, the God who saw me in the wilderness sees you in yours.
Your pain hasn't gone unnoticed. Your tears have been counted.

My Advice to You

You are not defined by what was done to you. Your identity comes from God, not your situation. **When God calls you by name, believe Him.** He sees you as whole, even if others see you as broken. **The**

wilderness is not the end. Sometimes it's where you find Him the most clearly.

Hold On To This

"You are the God who sees me… I have now seen the One who sees me." (Genesis 16:13)
"The Lord is close to the brokenhearted and saves those who are crushed in spirit." (Psalm 34:18). *"I have called you by name; you are Mine."* (Isaiah 43:1)

Remember this, you may be overlooked by people, but you are never unseen by God.

CHAPTER FIVE

Rebekah ~ I'm Coming to You as a Woman of Influence
How my choices shaped generations; for better or worse. (Genesis 24; 27)

"I'm coming to you as a woman to tell you not to try to force what God already promised."

I'm coming to you as a woman who learned the hard way. When the servant of Abraham found me at the well, I was eager, generous, and ready to step into God's plan. I married Isaac and became the mother of twins, Esau and Jacob. From the start, they were different, and I favored Jacob.

I had a good start. I was the girl who said yes when a stranger showed up, sent by God to find a wife for Isaac. I watered his camels, welcomed him into my family, and before I knew it, I was part of the covenant line.

God even spoke to me personally when I was pregnant, He told me I was carrying twins and that *the older would serve the younger* (Genesis 25:23). Friend, when God gives you a word like that, you hold it close.

Years later, my sons Esau and Jacob grew into men. Isaac loved Esau more, and I loved Jacob.
One day, I overheard Isaac getting ready to bless Esau. My heart started racing, I remembered God's promise, and I thought, *"This is it. I've got to make sure Jacob gets it."*

So I came up with a plan. I told Jacob to pretend to be his brother, dress in Esau's clothes, cover his arms with goat skin, and serve Isaac a meal so he'd think it was Esau and bless him instead.

It worked… but it wrecked my family. Jacob had to flee for his life. Esau hated him. And I never saw Jacob again.

When it came time for the blessing, I schemed. I coached Jacob to deceive his father and take what God had already promised him. Yes, the blessing came to pass, but my way brought pain, separation, and years of loss.

Friend, I'm just coming to you as a woman who has learned the hard way, God's plan doesn't need my manipulation. It may not be stealing a birthright but it could be, trying to control every outcome, meddling in situations or micromanaging relationships
My interference didn't speed up His promise; it cost me relationships, peace, and time I could never get back.

I thought I was helping God.
But in reality, I was saying, *"I don't trust you to handle this without me."*

Friend, your influence is powerful. You can use it to nurture God's plan, or to push it through in your timing. Be careful, even if your goal is right, the wrong method can leave scars. Influence is a gift; wield it with prayer, not manipulation.

What I Want You to Know

You may feel the urge to step in, to "make things happen," especially when you see time slipping away. But if God promised it, it will come to pass without you breaking trust, bending truth, or crossing lines.

My Advice to You

Trust God's process as much as His promise. Don't manipulate what you should be praying over. Don't let urgency push you into disobedience.

Hold On To This

"Be still, and know that I am God." (Psalm 46:10). "The blessing of the Lord makes one rich, and He adds no sorrow with it." (Proverbs 10:22). "Commit your way to the Lord; trust in Him, and He will act." (Psalm 37:5)

I'm coming to you as a woman who tried to help God... and made a mess instead. Let Him write the story without your shortcuts.

CHAPTER SIX

Leah ~ I'm Coming to You as a Woman Who Learned to Praise
Finding joy even when you feel overlooked. (Genesis 29–30)

"I'm coming to you as a woman who knows what it's like to be unwanted by people but chosen by God."

I'm coming to you as a woman approved by God. I was the wife Jacob didn't choose. My father's deception put me in his tent, but his heart was always with my sister, Rachel. I gave him sons, but my soul longed for his love.

I didn't ask for this. I didn't ask to be part of a love triangle. I didn't ask to be compared to my younger sister every time I walked into a room.

But my father, Laban, had his own plan. On my wedding night, he sent me to Jacob instead of Rachel. And friends… Jacob wasn't blind. He knew he had been tricked, and from that moment on, I knew where I stood. I was the wife he didn't want.

Every day I saw the way Jacob looked at Rachel. His laughter was louder with her. His touch lingered longer. I was there cooking meals, keeping house, bearing children, but I was invisible to his heart.

And, I tried everything to win his affection. Every son I bore, I thought, *"Maybe now my husband will love me."*
Reuben. Simeon. Levi. And yet… nothing changed.

It took years for me to realize that God had been watching me the whole time. *"When the Lord saw that Leah was unloved, He enabled her to have children."* (Genesis 29:31)

Friend, that changed everything.
The moment I stopped trying to be chosen by a man and started praising the One who had already chosen me, I found peace. When I birthed my fourth son, Judah, I said, *"This time I will praise the Lord."*

Judah's line became the line of kings… the line of Jesus. The wife Jacob didn't choose became part of the story God had been writing all along.

At first, every child I bore was an attempt to earn his affection. But by the time I had Judah, I said, "This time, I will praise the Lord." That shift changed everything. My worth wasn't in Jacob's eyes anymore, it was in God's.

I'm Just Coming to You as a Woman

who knows the ache of being overlooked, undervalued, and unloved by the one you wanted to love you back but who also knows the joy of realizing you were never overlooked by God. Who knows about comparison, being overlooked and people-pleasing. Maybe you've been competing for someone's attention, approval, or affection. But your identity isn't in who chooses you, it's in the God who made you. And when you praise Him for who He is, not what you get, you'll find the peace you've been searching for.

What I Want You to Know

Stop living for someone's approval that they may never give you. Your value isn't measured by human affection, it's defined by divine selection. Sometimes God allows you to be hidden in the eyes of people so He can reveal you in His plan.

Hold On To This

"When my father and my mother forsake me, then the Lord will take me up." (Psalm 27:10). *"You are precious in my sight, and honored, and I love you."* (Isaiah 43:4). *"The stone which the builders rejected has become the chief cornerstone."* (Psalm 118:22)

I'm coming to you as a woman to tell you to stop crying over who didn't choose you and start praising the God who already has.

CHAPTER SEVEN

Rachel ~ I'm Coming to You as a Woman Who Waited and Wept
Holding hope when your heart feels empty. (Genesis 29–30; 35:16–20)

"Friends don't let pretty fool you, beauty doesn't cancel battles."

I'm coming to you as a woman who had everything people said would make me happy… but it still wasn't enough.

People looked at me and saw beauty. They saw the sparkle in my eyes, the way Jacob worked 14 years for me, the way my presence drew attention. On the outside, my life seemed perfect.

But beauty didn't keep me from envy. Love didn't protect me from longing. Marriage didn't shield me from pain.

I had Jacob's love, but not the children I longed for. Every time Leah bore another son, my heart broke. I cried out to Jacob in desperation, "Give me children, or I'll die!"(Genesis 30:1) But only God could open my womb.

While my sister Leah bore son after son, my arms remained empty. And I'll be honest with you, it ate me alive. I watched her give Jacob the one thing I couldn't give him, and my heart screamed, *"Why not me, Lord?"*

But what I didn't realize at the time was that children were not the cure for my soul's ache. I was looking for my worth in what I could produce, rather than resting in the God who gave me worth before I ever produced a thing.

Eventually, God remembered me. He opened my womb, and I gave birth to Joseph. Later, I had Benjamin. But, by the time I held my second son, my story was already winding to its end.

I learned too late that no amount of outward blessings can fill the emptiness of an unhealed heart. If your joy depends on the next thing you want God to give you, you'll miss the beauty of what He's already placed in your life.

Years later, he did. Joseph's cry healed years of silent tears. And though my life ended giving birth to Benjamin, I left this earth knowing God had heard me.

I'm Just Coming to You as a Woman

To tell you that you may be in a season where what you've prayed for still hasn't come. You may suffer with social media comparisons or envying someone else's life without knowing their pain.

But, don't let bitterness consume you. God hears every tear, and His timing will be perfect. And when He answers, it will be worth the wait. I'm just coming to you as a woman who knows what it's like to be admired but still feel insecure. To have what others want but still feel like it's not enough. To get the blessing you prayed for and still realize there's a deeper need in your soul only God can fill.

What I Want You to Know

Don't compare your season to someone else's, comparison will poison your gratitude. What you think will "finally make you happy" often won't, unless your heart is anchored in God first. Your identity can't be rooted in what you can produce; it must be rooted in who God says you are.

Hold On To This

"Charm is deceitful, and beauty is vain, but a woman who fears the Lord is to be praised." (Proverbs 31:30). "Delight yourself in the Lord, and He will give you the desires of your heart." (Psalm 37:4). "The Lord is my shepherd; I shall not want." (Psalm 23:1)

I'm coming to you as a woman to tell you not to spend your whole life chasing "the next thing" and miss the God who is already everything.

CHAPTER EIGHT

Tamar ~ I'm Coming to You as a Woman fighting for my place in promise
How my choices shaped generations for better or worse. (Genesis 38; Matthew 1:3)

" I'm coming to you as a woman who refused to let my story be erased."

I'm coming to you as a woman, whose name may come with controversy. My name is Tamar. I was married into the family of Judah, yes, the Judah from whom kings would one day come. I married his first son, Er. But he was wicked, and the Lord took his life.
By law, Judah's second son, Onan, was supposed to marry me and give me children so my husband's name wouldn't disappear from Israel. But he refused to give me an heir and the Lord took his life too.

Judah promised me his third son, Shelah, when he was grown.
So I waited… and waited.
But when the time came, Judah didn't keep his word. I was left alone, childless, and without protection, which, in my time, meant without a future.

I could have accepted the silence and shame. But something in me knew this wasn't how my story was meant to end.

I heard Judah was traveling to shear his sheep. I covered my face with a veil, dressed like a prostitute, and waited where he would pass. He didn't recognize me. We agreed on payment, and I asked for his seal, cord, and staff as a pledge.
We were together, and I conceived.

When word came that I was pregnant, Judah was ready to have me burned until I sent his seal, cord, and staff to him. He realized the truth: *"She is more righteous than I, since I wouldn't give her to my son Shelah."*

I gave birth to twin sons, Perez and Zerah.
Perez would become part of the lineage of King David and eventually, Jesus the Messiah.

I wasn't perfect. My methods were bold and controversial. But I fought for my rightful place in the covenant family. And God, in His sovereignty, used my determination to preserve the promise.

I'm Just Coming to You as a Woman

who knows that sometimes you have to contend for the place God has already given you. Don't let anyone's neglect or broken promise erase your inheritance.

What I Want You to Know

Sometimes courage looks like taking an uncomfortable stand. People's rejection does not cancel God's promise. God can redeem even the most complicated situations for His glory.

Hold On To This

"She is more righteous than I." (Genesis 38:26). *"The stone the builders rejected has become the cornerstone."* (Psalm 118:22). *"For the gifts and the calling of God are irrevocable."* (Romans 11:29)

I'm coming to you as a woman to tell you don't let fear or shame convince you that your story is over. God's plan for your life is bigger than people's failure to keep their word.

PART II

Exodus & Wilderness (Deliverance & Law)

As God's chosen people multiplied in Egypt, women played key roles in deliverance. Their courage and song carried hope through slavery, plagues, and wilderness wandering.

CHAPTER NINE

Shiphrah ~ I'm Coming to You as a Woman Who Defied Pharaoh
Courage When It Could Cost You Everything (Exodus 1:15–21)

"I'm coming to you as a woman who chose to fear God more than I feared a king."

I'm coming to you as a woman named Shiphrah, and I was one of the Hebrew midwives in Egypt. My work was sacred. I helped bring new life into the world. But then came a decree from Pharaoh himself: *Kill the Hebrew baby boys as soon as they are born.* It was more than a command, it was a death sentence for a generation.

Along with my fellow midwife, Puah, I had to decide: obey Pharaoh or obey God.
We knew what would happen if we defied the king, it could cost us our lives. But we also knew what would happen if we obeyed, we'd be participating in destroying our own people. We chose to fear God. We told Pharaoh that the Hebrew women gave birth too quickly for us to arrive in time. And because of that choice, the boys lived, including one named Moses.

I didn't know then that the baby whose life was spared would grow up to confront Pharaoh and lead our people out of Egypt. Sometimes your courage doesn't just save the moment, it shapes the future.

I'm Just Coming to You as a Woman

Who knows that there will be moments when obeying God will put you at odds with the people in power. But when those moments come, remember: earthly kings may punish, but the King of Kings rewards.

What I Want You to Know

Fear of God will keep you steady when the fear of man tries to shake you. Doing the right thing may cost you now, but it pays eternal dividends. Your quiet obedience can become the foundation for someone else's deliverance.

Hold On To This

"The midwives, however, feared God and did not do what the king of Egypt had told them to do; they let the boys live." (Exodus 1:17). *"We must obey God rather than human beings!"* (Acts 5:29). *"Be strong and courageous. Do not be afraid… for the Lord your God will be with you wherever you go."* (Joshua 1:9)

I'm coming to you as a woman to tell you that courage isn't the absence of fear, it's the choice to fear God more. When you stand for life, truth, and righteousness, you stand with Him.

CHAPTER TEN

Puah ~ I'm Coming to You as a Woman Who Protected Life
Standing Bold in the Face of Injustice (Exodus 1:15–21)

"I'm coming to you as a woman who refused to be silent when the command was wrong."

I'm coming to you as a woman, named Puah. You may not hear my name as often, but I stood side by side with my sister who you just heard from, Shiphrah. We were Hebrew midwives in Egypt, and our work was holy, helping mothers bring life into the world. But one day, Pharaoh called us in and gave a command that made my stomach turn: *Kill the Hebrew baby boys when they're born.*

It was a moment where the choice was clear, obey the earthly king or obey the King of Heaven. Shiphrah and I looked at each other and knew we couldn't do it. We feared God more than we feared Pharaoh. So we let the boys live. When Pharaoh demanded to know why, we told him the truth in a way that preserved our lives: *"The Hebrew women are vigorous and give birth before we arrive."* It was our way of resisting without drawing a sword. Our weapon was obedience to God.

God honored our courage. Not only did He spared us, but He gave us families of our own, a blessing for women who had spent years helping others deliver children.
And because those boys lived, the deliverer of Israel, Moses, would be born and grow to lead our people out of slavery.

I'm Just Coming to You as a Woman

Who knows what it's like to be given an order that goes against everything God stands for and having to choose whether you'll stand with truth or bow to fear.

What I Want You to Know

Silence in the face of injustice is agreement. You can resist evil without hatred, but you cannot resist without courage. God rewards obedience, even when it's costly.

Hold On To This

"The midwives, however, feared God and did not do what the king of Egypt had told them to do; they let the boys live." (Exodus 1:17). *"Be strong and courageous. Do not be afraid… for the Lord your God will be with you wherever you go."* (Joshua 1:9). *"Do not be overcome by evil, but overcome evil with good."* (Romans 12:21)

I'm coming to you as a woman to tell you that you don't need a sword in your hand to be a warrior.

Sometimes, your courage to obey God is the battle cry that changes history.

CHAPTER ELEVEN

Jochebed ~ I'm Coming to You as a Mother Who Hid a Deliverer
Trusting God with the child you can't protect yourself. (Exodus 2:1–10; Hebrews 11:23)

"I'm coming to you as a woman who had to release what I loved most and trust God to protect it."

I'm coming to you as a woman, who knows what it is like to trust God with your children. When I held my son for the first time, I knew he was special. I can't explain it, it wasn't just a mother's love, it was a holy knowing. But the timing of his birth was dangerous. Pharaoh had commanded that every Hebrew baby boy be killed. My heart was torn between fear and faith.

For three months, I hid him. Every cry made me nervous. Every knock at the door made my heart pound. I did everything I could to protect him, but there came a moment when I knew my arms weren't enough.

I hid Moses as long as I could, then placed him in a basket on the Nile. I didn't abandon him, I entrusted him to God. And He brought my baby back to me under Pharaoh's roof.

There's a kind of love that wants to hold tight. But there's a kind of faith that knows when to let go. I made a basket, covered it with tar, and placed my precious baby into the Nile River. My hands trembled, but my spirit whispered, *"Lord, I place him in Yours now."*

That was the hardest thing I've ever done, not because I didn't love him, but because I loved him enough to surrender him to the One who could do more for him than I ever could.

I didn't know that Pharaoh's own daughter would find him. I didn't know she would adopt him as her son. And I surely didn't know God would arrange it so I could nurse my own child under her protection.

That's how God works. When you release something into His hands, He can return it to you with greater provision and purpose.

I'm Just Coming to You as a Woman

Who has learned that surrender isn't giving up, it's giving over. When you can't see how it will work out, trust that the same God who formed what you love, can protect and position it better than you can. When you can't protect your promise, place it in the river of God's care. He knows how to return it in ways you can't imagine.

What I Want You to Know

Sometimes the safest place for what you love is not in your arms, but in God's care.
Surrender is an act of faith, not failure. When you trust God with what's precious, He can position it for His glory.

Hold On To This

"By faith Moses' parents hid him for three months after he was born… and they were not afraid of the king's edict." (Hebrews 11:23). *"Cast your cares on the Lord and He will sustain you."* (Psalm 55:22). *"The Lord will watch over your coming and going both now and forevermore."* (Psalm 121:8)

I'm coming to you as a woman to tell you that sometimes the bravest thing you can do is place what you love most into the river and trust God to carry it where it's meant to go.

CHAPTER TWELVE

Miriam ~ I'm Coming to You as a Woman Who Sang of Victory
Celebrating God's deliverance on the other side of the sea. (Exodus 2:4–8; 15:20–21; Numbers 12)

"Friend, your gift is powerful — but pride can make it poisonous."

I'm coming to you as a woman who was called, gifted, and anointed… but almost let pride ruin it all.

When I was young, I was bold. I was the one who watched over my baby brother Moses as he floated in that basket down the Nile. I had the courage to approach Pharaoh's daughter and make sure my mother could nurse him. Even as a girl, I was a protector, a leader in the making.

Years later, when God brought Israel out of Egypt, I stood with a tambourine in my hand, singing the song of deliverance:
"Sing to the Lord, for He has triumphed gloriously; the horse and rider He has thrown into the sea!" (Exodus 15:21)
The joy was real. The calling was clear. God had placed me in leadership alongside my brothers, Moses and Aaron.

But here's what I need you to hear, just because God uses you doesn't mean your heart can't trip you up. There came a time when I didn't like the way God was leading through Moses. I thought, *"Does God only speak through him? Doesn't He also speak through me?"* (Numbers 12:2)

It started as a thought. Then it became a whisper. Then it turned into public criticism.

And before I knew it, I was standing in rebellion against the very God who had raised me up.

God heard my words. And His response? He struck me with leprosy. In an instant, my skin turned white as snow, and I was put out of the camp for seven days.

Seven days of shame. Seven days of isolation. Seven days to think about how quickly a pure calling can be tainted by an impure heart.

It was only by God's mercy and Moses' prayer that I was restored.

Worship isn't just what you do when you get the answer, it's how you declare God's glory so everyone knows He did it.

I'm Just Coming to You as a Woman

who knows the thrill of being used by God… and the sting of being corrected by Him. It's possible to dance in the anointing one moment and be disciplined in the next. Leadership is not just about the songs you sing, the people you inspire, or the victories you celebrate, it's about staying humble enough to remember who the true Leader is.

Don't hold back your song. Let your victory be loud enough to encourage someone still waiting for their breakthrough. Lead well but don't let your attitude or offense get in the way.

What I Want You to Know

Don't let your gift blind you to your need for humility. If God puts someone else in a position you thought you should have, trust His wisdom over your feelings. When correction comes, receive it, it's a sign God still has plans for you.

Hold On To This

"God opposes the proud but gives grace to the humble." (James 4:6). *"Humble yourselves before the Lord, and He will lift you up."* (James 4:10). *"Let nothing be done through selfish ambition or conceit, but in lowliness of mind let each esteem others better than himself."* (Philippians 2:3)

I'm coming to you as a woman to tell you not to let pride talk you out of your position. Stay small in your own eyes, no matter how big God makes your platform.

CHAPTER THIRTEEN

Zipporah ~ I'm Coming to You as a Woman Who Stood in the Gap
Obedience When It's Hard to Understand (Exodus 2:21; 4:24–26)

"I'm coming to you as a woman who had to act quickly, even when I didn't fully understand the why; and it saved my family."

I'm coming to you as a woman named Zipporah, daughter of Jethro, priest of Midian.
I met Moses when he fled Egypt and ended up at our well. My father welcomed him, and I became his wife. We had two sons and lived a quiet life until God called Moses to return to Egypt and set His people free.

On the way to Egypt, something strange and terrifying happened. The Lord confronted Moses and it became clear that our family was in danger because our son had not been circumcised according to the covenant God gave Abraham. I didn't have time for a deep theological discussion. I acted. I took a flint knife, circumcised my son, and touched Moses' feet with the blood. Then God let him go.

I didn't fully grasp everything in that moment. I just knew this: when God requires something, delayed obedience is dangerous. It wasn't a pleasant task. It wasn't the kind of act you dream of doing for your family. But it was necessary and it saved Moses' life so he could go on to fulfill his calling.

I'm Just Coming to You as a Woman

who knows that sometimes obedience will make you uncomfortable. It will ask you to act fast, to do things that may not make sense in the moment, and to trust that God knows why He's asking it. Your willingness to obey could be the very thing that protects your family's destiny.

What I Want You to Know

Obedience is urgent and delayed obedience can cost more than you realize. God's instructions are for your good, even when they're hard to carry out. Your actions can protect the calling on your household.

Hold On To This

"At a lodging place on the way, the Lord met Moses and was about to kill him. But Zipporah took a flint knife, cut off her son's foreskin and touched Moses' feet with it." (Exodus 4:24-25)

"To obey is better than sacrifice, and to heed is better than the fat of rams." (1 Samuel 15:22)

"Trust in the Lord with all your heart and lean not on your own understanding." (Proverbs 3:5)

I'm coming to you as a woman to tell you not to wait to obey when God speaks. Sometimes your quick obedience will save more than just your life it will preserve the future God has planned for you and those you love.

PART III

Judges Era (Before the Kings)

In the days before Israel had kings, women rose up with unexpected courage. When leaders faltered, God used their wisdom, bravery, and strength to deliver His people.

CHAPTER FOURTEEN

Deborah ~ I'm Coming to You as a Woman Who Led Boldly
Stepping into courage when the battle calls. (Judges 4–5)

"Friend, don't shrink when God says stand tall."

"I'm coming to you as a woman who led in a man's world, but never stopped listening to God." When my story begins, Israel was in trouble. We were being crushed under the hand of King Jabin, and his commander Sisera had nine hundred iron chariots. The people were afraid, discouraged, and spiritually cold.

And God? He chose me, a wife, a prophetess, a judge to lead.
Yes… *me*.

I judged Israel under the shade of my palm tree, but when God called us to war, I didn't hesitate. Barak refused to go without me, so I went. I wasn't there for the glory; I was there for the victory God promised.

I know what it feels like to be in a space where it's "not normal" for you to lead. Some folks didn't expect to see a woman sitting under the palm tree, judging disputes, giving counsel, and delivering God's word to the nation.

But I learned something early: if God calls you, the setting doesn't have to fit *you just have to obey*. When the Lord told me to call Barak and give him instructions for battle, I spoke exactly what God said:
"Has not the Lord, the God of Israel, commanded you…?" (Judges 4:6)

Barak believed me but he also said, *"I'll only go if you go with me."* And I told him, "I'll go, but the honor will not be yours, the Lord will deliver Sisera into the hands of a woman."

That wasn't arrogance. That was prophecy. And it came to pass exactly as God said. Jael, another woman, was the one who brought the final blow to the enemy.

Leadership isn't about titles; it's about obedience. When God calls you to stand up, do it, even if you're the only one willing. I didn't fight the battle alone. God paired my prophetic voice with Barak's military skill. That's something I need you to hear: Don't confuse leadership with doing *everything* yourself. Sometimes God will join your gift with someone else's so the victory is complete.

After the victory, I didn't just move on to the next challenge. I *sang*. Judges 5 is a whole chapter of praise, a song about what God did, how He fought for us, and how the willing hearts of the people made the difference. That song still lives on because gratitude cements victory in the memory of God's people.

I'm Just Coming to You as a Woman

who has stood in the tension of leading with authority while walking in humility. Leadership will test your courage, your patience, and your obedience, but if you keep your ear to God's voice, you'll not only lead well… you'll lead with joy.

What I Want You to Know

You are never "out of place" if you are standing where God put you. Leadership isn't a solo mission so value the people God connects to your purpose. Celebrate every victory; worship seals the testimony.

Hold On To This

"The Lord gave the word; great was the company of those who proclaimed it." (Psalm 68:11). *"The steps of a good person are ordered by the Lord, and He delights in their way."* (Psalm 37:23). *"Trust in the Lord with all your heart… and He will direct your paths."* (Proverbs 3:5–6)

I'm coming to you as a woman to tell you to lead boldly, sing loudly, and let your life be the kind of victory song others can join in on.

CHAPTER FIFTEEN

Jael ~ I'm Coming to You as a Woman Who Finished the Fight
When the moment comes, drive the nail in. (Judges 4:17–22; 5:24–27)

"I'm coming to you as a woman who saw the enemy coming and refused to let him leave alive."

"I'm coming to you as a woman named Jael".
I wasn't an Israelite, but I lived near them. My people had a peace treaty with King Jabin, the oppressor of Israel. That meant I wasn't supposed to pick a side in their battles.
But when the commander of his army, Sisera, came to my tent running for his life, I knew whose side I was on.

Sisera fled after Deborah and Barak led Israel to victory. He came alone, exhausted, desperate, looking for a place to hide. He thought my tent was safe because of my husband's treaty with him.

I welcomed him in, covered him with a blanket, and gave him milk when he asked for water. His eyes grew heavy, and soon, he fell into a deep sleep.

I could have let him rest and slip away later. But I knew this man was the enemy of God's people. If I let him live, he would rise again to oppress.

So I took a tent peg in one hand and a hammer in the other. With one decisive blow, I drove the peg through his temple into the ground.

When Barak came looking for him, I showed him the body. That day, God used my hands to bring peace to Israel.

I'm Just Coming to You as a Woman

who knows that sometimes God puts the victory in your hands but you still have to take the swing. Courage doesn't always look like standing on a battlefield; sometimes it looks like seizing the moment in your own home. Your hands may not hold a tent peg, but God may place an enemy in your path that only you can take down. Don't shrink back. Finish what He puts in front of you.

What I Want You to Know

God can use unlikely people to win great victories. The tools you have are enough when you put them in God's hands. Courage is often a quiet, decisive act that changes everything.

Hold On To This

"Most blessed of women be Jael, the wife of Heber the Kenite, most blessed of tent-dwelling women." (Judges 5:24). *"Be strong and take heart, all you who hope in the Lord."* (Psalm 31:24). *"Do not be afraid; do not be discouraged, for the Lord your God will be with you wherever you go."* (Joshua 1:9)

I'm coming to you as a woman to tell you that you may not have a sword, but you have something in your hands that God can use to take down the enemy. Don't be afraid to act

PART IV

Conquest & Settlement (Joshua, Judges, Ruth)

As the land was conquered and families rebuilt, women stood at crossroads of faith and failure. Some chose covenant, others comfort and their decisions echo to this day.

CHAPTER SIXTEEN

Rahab ~ I'm Coming to You as a Woman Redeemed
Your past doesn't disqualify you from God's future. (Joshua 2; 6:22–25; Matthew 1:5)

"I'm coming to you as a woman who didn't let her past decide her future."

"I'm coming to you as a woman who knows what it is like to have a bad reputation". When people in Jericho spoke my name, they didn't say it kindly. They called me *Rahab the prostitute*. My reputation was known. My past was public. And if you had told me back then that God would use me to help deliver His people and place me in the lineage of the Messiah I might've laughed in disbelief.

But, God specializes in rewriting stories.

They called me "Rahab the prostitute," but when I heard about Israel's God, I believed. I hid the spies, marked my window with scarlet, and my family was saved when Jericho fell.

When two Israelite spies came to my city, word got out fast. The king's men came looking for them, but I hid them on my roof under stalks of flax.

Why?
Because I had heard about their God, the God who split the Red Sea, the God who gave His people victory over kings. And deep down, I believed He was the true God of heaven and earth.

I made a choice: to align myself with God's people, even if it meant risking my life.

I didn't just believe, I acted. I lied to the king's messengers to protect the spies, then made a bold request:
"Swear to me by the Lord that you will show kindness to my family, because I have shown kindness to you." (Joshua 2:12)

They agreed, and gave me a sign, a scarlet cord to hang from my window so my household would be spared when Israel attacked.

When the walls of Jericho fell, my house stood. My family was safe. And I was brought into Israel not as an outcast, but as one redeemed.

My name is no longer just "Rahab the prostitute." My name is written in the lineage of Jesus Christ (Matthew 1:5) and in the hall of faith (Hebrews 11:31).

I'm Just Coming to You as a Woman

who knows what it's like to live with a label, but also what it's like to be renamed by God. Your past is not a prison, it's the platform where God can show His mercy and power. Friend, your past may be written in people's memory, but God writes a new name over you. Walk in the future He's given you.

What I Want You to Know

Faith isn't just what you believe, it's what you do with what you believe. God can use anyone who is willing to trust Him, no matter their past. One act of courage can change the future for generations.

Hold On To This

"By faith the prostitute Rahab, because she welcomed the spies, was not killed with those who were disobedient." (Hebrews 11:31). *"If anyone is in Christ, he is a new creation; the old has gone, the new is here!"* (2 Corinthians 5:17). *"Those who look to Him are radiant; their faces are never covered with shame."* (Psalm 34:5)

I'm coming to you as a woman to tell you that your faith today can break the cycle of your past and open the door to a whole new future.

CHAPTER SEVENTEEN

Delilah ~ I'm Coming to You as a Woman Who Misused Her Power
The danger of influence without godly wisdom. (Judges 16:4–22)

"I'm coming to you as a woman who learned that when you trade trust for gain, everybody loses."

I'm coming to you as a woman who when people hear my name, they remember the woman who brought down Samson, the man with supernatural strength.
But, I'm here to tell you the truth behind the whispers.

Samson trusted me with his heart, but I sold it for silver. My manipulation cost him his strength and his life.

The Philistine rulers came to me with an offer:
"Find out the secret of his strength, and we'll give you silver."

Silver. Power. Influence. It all sounded tempting. And if I'm being real, part of me felt like I was the one in control. After all, I knew Samson's weaknesses. I knew how he loved me.

So I used my position in his life not to protect him, but to probe him. I kept pressing him until he revealed the truth that his strength came from being set apart from God as a Nazarite, never cutting his hair.

Once I had the answer, I sold it. I cut off the very thing God had marked in him. And when the Philistines captured him, the victory didn't feel sweet. It felt hollow.

I got what I thought I wanted, but lost something much greater than my integrity.

I'm just coming to you as a woman

who knows what it's like to let greed, pressure, or personal gain push you into destroying someone else's calling and your own peace.

The enemy will always pay you to betray what's holy. But the payout can't cover the cost to your soul. Influence is a gift. If you use it for selfish gain, it will destroy more than you can see. Seek God before you seek advantage.

What I Want You to Know

Don't let the promise of gain make you blind to the cost of compromise. Relationships are sacred, guard the trust God allows you to hold. Your influence can be used to build or to break, choose wisely.

Hold On To This

"What good will it be for someone to gain the whole world, yet forfeit their soul?" (Matthew 16:26). *"Do not be deceived: God cannot be mocked. A man reaps what he sows."* (Galatians 6:7). *"Above all else, guard your heart, for everything you do flows from it."* (Proverbs 4:23)

I'm coming to you as a woman to tell you not to sell out your calling or someone else's destiny for a temporary reward. The cost is too high.

CHAPTER EIGHTEEN

Hannah ~ I'm coming to you as a woman who prayed through the pain
"Don't let the pain stop your prayer life." (1 Samuel 1–2)

"I'm coming to you as a woman who cried until her voice was gone, yet found peace before the answer came."

I'm coming to you as a woman who knows what it's like to want something so badly it aches. This could be people misunderstanding your struggle or mocking your dreams. For me, it was a child. Year after year, I watched other women hold their babies while my arms stayed empty. I smiled on the outside, but inside I was breaking.

And to make it worse, Peninnah, my husband's other wife, never missed a chance to remind me of what I didn't have. Her words cut deep, and the shame tried to settle into my bones.

One year, I couldn't take it anymore. I went to the temple and poured my soul out before God. My lips moved, but no sound came. I wasn't praying a pretty, polished prayer, I was giving Him my raw, unfiltered heart.

Eli, the priest, thought I was drunk. I told him, *"I have been pouring out my soul before the Lord."* (1 Samuel 1:15)

Sometimes people will misunderstand your desperation, but God never does.

In my prayer, I made a vow:
"Lord, if You give me a son, I'll give him back to You all the days of his life."

I didn't know when or how He would do it, but I left that temple with a strange peace. I had been heard.

And in time, the Lord remembered me. I gave birth to Samuel and when the time came, I kept my vow. I placed my miracle into the Lord's service. It was the hardest and most beautiful obedience I've ever walked in.

I'm Coming to You as a Woman

who knows the pain of delay, the sting of comparison, and the fight to keep believing when your womb, whether physical or spiritual, feels empty.

What I Want You to Know

God can handle your unpolished, tear-soaked prayers. A surrendered heart is a magnet for God's miracles. Sometimes the answer is not just for you, it's for God's glory and others' deliverance.

Hold On To This

"The Lord is close to the brokenhearted and saves those who are crushed in spirit." (Psalm 34:18). *"Delight yourself in the Lord, and He will give you the desires of your heart."* (Psalm 37:4). *"For this child I prayed, and the Lord has granted me my petition that I made to Him."* (1 Samuel 1:27)

I'm just coming to you as a woman to tell you to keep praying, keep believing, and when God answers, be ready to give Him back what you prayed for.

CHAPTER NINETEEN

Peninnah ~ *I'm Coming to You as a Woman Who Provoked*
When Jealousy Steals Your Peace (1 Samuel 1:2–7)

"I'm coming to you as a woman who let insecurity turn me into someone I'm not proud of."

I'm coming to you as a woman named Peninnah. I was one of Elkanah's wives, the other just gave you her side of the story, Hannah. I had something she didn't: children. She had something I didn't: his deep, tender love.

Every year we went to Shiloh to worship and sacrifice. Every year, Elkanah gave me and my children our portion, but to Hannah, he gave a double portion because of his love for her.

It stung. I felt invisible even when I was in the same room. Instead of dealing with my hurt, I used my words to cut her down. I reminded her she was barren. I let my bitterness become my weapon. And yes, she wept because of me.

What I didn't understand was this: my worth was never in comparison to hers.
My blessings, my children, were gifts from God. But I let jealousy blind me to my own blessings. Hannah prayed through her pain and found favor with God. I could have prayed too. I could have asked God to heal my heart. But I chose competition over compassion.

I'm Just Coming to You as a Woman

who knows how dangerous it is to let comparison and insecurity rule your spirit.
If you're not careful, you'll become the antagonist in someone else's story while missing the beauty of your own.

What I Want You to Know

Jealousy will steal your peace and poison your relationships. There's room for every woman to be loved and valued in God's Kingdom. Gratitude is the cure for comparison.

Hold On To This

"A heart at peace gives life to the body, but envy rots the bones." (Proverbs 14:30). *"Do nothing out of selfish ambition or vain conceit. Rather, in humility, value others above yourselves."* (Philippians 2:3). *"Rejoice with those who rejoice; mourn with those who mourn."* (Romans 12:15)

I'm coming to you as a woman to tell you not to let jealousy write your story. There's too much God has for you to waste energy competing with someone He also loves.

CHAPTER TWENTY

Orpah ~ I'm Coming to You as a Woman Who Turned Back
Choosing comfort over covenant changed my story. (Ruth 1:4–14)

"I'm coming to you as a woman who chose the familiar over the unknown and I still think about what could have been."

I'm coming to you as a woman named Orpah. I married into Naomi's family when they came to Moab during the famine. I loved my husband, but our time together was short, death came for him just as it came for his brother and father.

That left me, my sister-in-law Ruth, and our mother-in-law Naomi; three widows with no clear future.

When Naomi decided to go back to Bethlehem, Ruth and I started the journey with her. But somewhere on that road, Naomi stopped and told us to return to our mothers' homes. She said she had nothing left to give us; no sons, no security.

I wept. I loved Naomi. But I also knew that going with her meant leaving behind everything familiar: my culture, my language, my gods, my people.

I kissed her goodbye and turned back toward Moab. *I went back to what I knew, and my name faded from the story.*

Ruth didn't turn back.
She clung to Naomi and stepped into a story neither of us could have imagined; a story that would lead her to Boaz, to redemption, and into the lineage of King David and the Messiah Himself.

I'm not here to tell you I made the right choice. I'm here to tell you that fear of the unknown can make you walk away from a divine appointment.

I'm Just Coming to You as a Woman

who wants you to think carefully before you walk away from something hard just because it's unfamiliar. The path that stretches your faith might also be the path to your destiny. The easy road may seem safe, but it may also lead you away from destiny.

What I Want You to Know

Comfort zones can be cages if God is calling you out of them. Not all who start the journey will finish it but you can decide which one you'll be. Destiny often hides on the other side of uncertainty.

Hold On To This

"But Ruth clung to her. 'Look,' said Naomi, 'your sister-in-law is going back to her people and her gods. Go back with her.'" (Ruth 1:14–15). *"Trust in the Lord with all your heart and lean not on your own understanding."* (Proverbs 3:5). *"No one who puts a hand to the plow and looks back is fit for service in the kingdom of God."* (Luke 9:62)

I'm coming to you as a woman to tell you not to let the fear of what you can't see keep you from the blessing God has already set in motion. The road may be uncertain, but the One who calls you will not fail you.

CHAPTER TWENTY-ONE

Ruth ~ I'm Coming to You as a Woman Who Chose Covenant
Leaving comfort to walk into God's plan. (Ruth 1–4; Matthew 1:5)

"I'm coming to you as a woman who left everything familiar to follow God's leading and found more than I ever imagined."

I'm coming to you as a woman named Ruth. I was born in Moab, a land outside the covenant of Israel. I didn't grow up knowing the God of Abraham, Isaac, and Jacob. But I married into a family that did.
And then famine, death, and grief came. My husband died. My father-in-law died. My brother-in-law died.

All that was left was me, my sister-in-law Orpah, and my mother-in-law Naomi.

Naomi decided to return to her home in Bethlehem. She urged both Orpah and me to go back to our own mothers and start over. Orpah kissed her goodbye. I didn't.

Something in me knew my place was with Naomi. My future was tied to hers. And more than that, my heart had come to believe in her God.

I told her, *"Where you go I will go, and where you stay I will stay. Your people will be my people and your God my God."*

That day, I left Moab behind; my culture, my idols, my comfort zone and stepped into an unknown future.

We arrived in Bethlehem with nothing, but God made a way. While gleaning in the fields to provide for us, I met Boaz, a man of honor who showed kindness to a foreign widow.
Through him, I found not just provision, but redemption. We married, and I gave birth to Obed, the grandfather of King David.
I didn't know it then, but I had stepped into the very lineage of the Messiah.

I'm Just Coming to You as a Woman

who wants you to know that faith will sometimes lead you away from everything safe but toward everything good. God can rewrite your story when you're willing to leave what's behind and follow Him into the unknown.

What I Want You to Know

Obedience often requires leaving comfort behind. Who you choose to walk with will shape your destiny. God can graft you into His plan no matter where you come from.

Hold On To This

"Where you go I will go, and where you stay I will stay. Your people will be my people and your God my God." (Ruth 1:16). "The Lord rewards your work, and your wages will be full from the Lord, the God of Israel, under whose wings you have come to seek refuge." (Ruth 2:12). "Forget the former things; do not dwell on the past. See, I am doing a new thing!" (Isaiah 43:18–19)

I'm coming to you as a woman to tell you that you may not see the full picture now, but trust the God who is leading you. What feels like leaving everything may be the very step into your destiny.

CHAPTER TWENTY-TWO

Naomi ~ I'm Coming to You as a Woman Who Returned
When bitterness turns back into joy. (Ruth 1–4)

"I'm coming to you as a woman who changed her name because I thought my story was over but God wasn't finished."

I'm coming to you as a woman who became bitter! My name is Naomi. Once, I had a husband, two sons, and a home in Bethlehem. Life felt secure. But a famine came, and we moved to Moab, a place far from my people and my God's temple.

In Moab, I lost my husband.
Then I lost both my sons.

Grief changes you.
I decided to go back to Bethlehem because I heard the famine had lifted. My daughters-in-law, Orpah and Ruth, started the journey with me, but I told them to return to their families. Orpah turned back. Ruth didn't.

By the time I arrived in Bethlehem, the women recognized me, but I told them, *"Don't call me Naomi (pleasant). Call me Mara (bitter), because the Almighty has made my life very bitter."*
I was convinced my future was empty.

Ruth, that loyal & determined young woman, was God's promise walking beside me.
Through her marriage to Boaz, my family line was restored. She gave me a grandson, Obed, who would become the grandfather of King David. And from that same line, generations later, the Messiah would come.

I thought I came home empty.
But God was already filling my life with more than I had lost.

I'm Just Coming to You as a Woman

who knows how it feels to believe the best is behind you.
But I need you to hear me: bitterness is not the end of your story. God knows how to bring joy back into places you thought were dead.

What I Want You to Know

God can turn your return into a restoration. Who you walk with matters so choose the ones who will walk you back into promise. Even in grief, your life is part of a bigger story.

Hold On To This

"Don't call me Naomi," she told them. "Call me Mara, because the Almighty has made my life very bitter." (Ruth 1:20). "Weeping may endure for a night, but joy comes in the morning." (Psalm 30:5). "Those who sow with tears will reap with songs of joy." (Psalm 126:5)

I'm coming to you as a woman to tell you not to rename yourself based on your worst season. The same God who sees your sorrow can write joy back into your story.

PART V

United & Divided Kingdoms (Samuel, Kings, Chronicles)

When kings ruled, the voices and choices of women shaped destinies. Some lifted nations toward God; others pulled them into idolatry and ruin. Their stories reveal both warning and wisdom.

CHAPTER TWENTY - THREE

Abigail ~ I'm Coming to You as a Woman of Wisdom
Responding to foolishness with grace and strategy. (1 Samuel 25)

"I'm coming to you as a woman who learned that one moment of courage can change the course of a whole household."

I'm coming to you as a woman who married a foolish man. I was married to a man named Nabal, his name literally meant "fool," and he lived up to it.
He was wealthy, but harsh and arrogant. His attitude made enemies easily.

One day, David, not yet king but already anointed, sent men to greet Nabal and ask for provisions during sheep-shearing time. It was a reasonable request; David's men had protected our flocks in the wilderness.

But Nabal insulted them, refused to help, and sent them away empty-handed.

When word reached David, his anger burned. He strapped on his sword and set out with four hundred men.
If he reached our home, every male in our household would be dead by morning.

Friend, I didn't have time to call a meeting or ask permission. I gathered bread, wine, roasted grain, meat, and figs. Then I rode out to meet David myself.

When I saw him, I bowed low and took the blame for my husband's offense. I reminded David of who he was, a man chosen by God and destined for the throne; and urged him not to shed innocent blood in a moment of rage.

My words calmed him. He thanked me for stopping him from avenging himself, for keeping him from sinning against God.

Soon after, God struck Nabal, and he died. David sent for me, and I became his wife. But my real victory wasn't the change in my marital status, it was knowing I had obeyed God, protected my household, and kept a future king from making a mistake.

I'm Just Coming to You as a Woman

who knows what it's like to live in a difficult marriage, to make quick decisions under pressure, and to use wisdom as a weapon. Sometimes the bravest thing you can do is step in and speak peace in the middle of someone else's anger.

What I Want You to Know

Wisdom is a form of courage, don't underestimate it. You can honor God even when the people closest to you don't. Your words can stop a disaster before it starts.

Hold On To This

"A gentle answer turns away wrath, but a harsh word stirs up anger." (Proverbs 15:1). *"Blessed are the peacemakers, for they will be called children of God."* (Matthew 5:9). *"The wise woman builds her house, but with her own hands the foolish one tears hers down."* (Proverbs 14:1)

I'm coming to you as a woman to tell you that in moments of conflict, choose wisdom over impulse. You might just save a life, a calling, or a future with one Spirit-led decision.

CHAPTER TWENTY-FOUR

Bathsheba ~ I'm Coming to You as a Woman Restored
From scandal to the mother of a king. (2 Samuel 11–12; 1 Kings 1–2)

"I'm coming to you as a woman who has lived through shame, loss, and grace; and saw God still keep His word."

I'm coming to you as a woman whose story began in shame when David called for me, but it didn't end there. God gave me Solomon, a son of peace, and secured his throne.

I didn't go looking for the moment that changed my life.
One day I was bathing in the privacy of my own courtyard. Next, I was summoned by King David. He wanted me and he got what he wanted.

When I found out I was pregnant, fear flooded my heart. I was married to Uriah, a loyal soldier in David's army. What followed was a series of events that spiraled out of control and ended with my husband's death.

I can't sugarcoat this, the sin was real, the grief was heavy, and the consequences were painful. The first child I bore from David died. My heart shattered.

But here's what I want you to hear: even in the middle of our worst failures, God doesn't abandon His purpose for us.

David repented. God restored him. And in time, I gave birth to another son, Solomon.
And God didn't just bless Solomon, He loved him. He chose him to build His temple. He made him king.

The same woman who walked through public scandal and deep loss became the mother of a king and part of the lineage of Jesus. That's what redemption looks like.

I'm Just Coming to You as a Woman

who knows what it's like to live under the shadow of past mistakes but still see the light of God's mercy. Your story doesn't end where you fell, it continues where God lifts you. Friend, your beginning doesn't define your ending. God can redeem any story.

What I Want You to Know

God's mercy can redeem even the messiest chapters of your life. Repentance opens the door to restoration. Your past doesn't cancel God's promise, it may just become the place He shows His grace the most.

Hold On To This

"Then David comforted his wife Bathsheba… she gave birth to a son, and they named him Solomon. The Lord loved him." (2 Samuel 12:24). "Blessed is the one whose transgressions are forgiven, whose sins are covered." (Psalm 32:1). "Where sin increased, grace increased all the more." (Romans 5:20)

I'm coming to you as a woman to tell you that your mistakes are not the end of your story. God's mercy can turn even your lowest moments into the foundation for His greatest promises.

CHAPTER TWENTY - FIVE

Tamar ~ *I'm Coming to You as a Woman Who Survived Violation*
When Your Voice Feels Stolen (2 Samuel 13:1–22)

"I'm coming to you as a woman who knows what it's like to be violated and then silenced."

I'm coming to you as a woman who was violated. My name is Tamar, daughter of King David. I lived in the royal palace, surrounded by the appearance of safety. I was beautiful, yes but I was also trusting, believing that my family was a place of protection.

My half-brother Amnon pretended to be sick and sent for me, saying he needed me to prepare food for him. I did not know he had planned this moment to take what was not his to take.

I told him no. I pleaded with him. But he overpowered me and forced himself on me. The moment it was over, he hated me more than he had claimed to love me. He threw me out. I tore my robe, put ashes on my head, and cried aloud. My brother Absalom told me to be quiet, to not take it to heart. My father, King David, was angry, but he did nothing.

So I lived in Absalom's house, desolate. Not because of the act alone, but because of the silence that followed. The absence of justice can wound as deeply as the wrong itself.

I'm Just Coming to You as a Woman

who wants you to know: what happened to you is not your fault. The shame is not yours to carry.
Your worth is not diminished by the evil done to you. And your voice matters, even if those around you don't want to hear it.

What I Want You to Know

Your body, your voice, your boundaries are God-given and must be honored. Silence does not heal wounds, light and truth do. God is a defender of the oppressed and will deal with injustice in His time.

Hold On To This

"The Lord is close to the brokenhearted and saves those who are crushed in spirit." (Psalm 34:18). "Speak up for those who cannot speak for themselves, for the rights of all who are destitute." (Proverbs 31:8). "He heals the brokenhearted and binds up their wounds." (Psalm 147:3)

I'm coming to you as a woman to tell you that what was done to you does not define you. God still calls you chosen, beloved, and whole. Your story is not over.

CHAPTER TWENTY - SIX

Rizpah ~ I'm Coming to You as a Woman Who Wouldn't Leave
Love that stands guard over the lost. (2 Samuel 21:8–14)

"I'm coming to you as a woman who stayed when it would have been easier to walk away."

I'm coming to you as a woman named Rizpah. I was a concubine of King Saul, the mother of two of his sons.
My life wasn't simple, I wasn't the queen, but I was still tangled in the politics of the palace. And when Saul's house fell, the consequences landed on my sons.

Because of Saul's actions against the Gibeonites, there was blood guilt on Israel. To make things right, King David allowed the Gibeonites to choose seven of Saul's descendants to be put to death.
Two of them were my boys.

They were executed and left exposed on the hill, according to the custom of the time. But I couldn't, I *wouldn't*, leave them there alone.

From the beginning of the barley harvest until the rains came, months, I stayed by their bodies. Day and night, I kept the birds away during the day and the wild animals away at night.
I didn't eat at banquets. I didn't go home. I sat on the rock in sackcloth. I refused to let their memory be dishonored, even if they were gone.

It wasn't comfortable. It wasn't glamorous. But it was love.
And my vigil caught the attention of the king. When David heard what I had done, he gathered the bones of my sons and of Saul and Jonathan, and gave them a proper burial.

I'm Just Coming to You as a Woman

who knows that sometimes the most powerful statement you can make is to *stay*.
Not every battle is loud, some are fought in silence, in persistence, and

in love that refuses to quit. Real love endures beyond convenience. It fights for dignity and honors even the broken places.

What I Want You to Know

Faithfulness speaks louder than words. Your persistence can move the hearts of leaders.
God sees your vigil, even when the world overlooks it.

Hold On To This

"Rizpah daughter of Aiah took sackcloth and spread it out for herself on a rock. From the beginning of the harvest till the rain poured down from the heavens on the bodies, she did not let the birds touch them by day or the wild animals by night." (2 Samuel 21:10). *"Let us not become weary in doing good, for at the proper time we will reap a harvest if we do not give up."* (Galatians 6:9). *"Blessed are those who mourn, for they will be comforted."* (Matthew 5:4)

I'm coming to you as a woman to tell you not to underestimate the power of simply standing your ground in love.

Sometimes staying is the loudest sermon you'll ever preach.

CHAPTER TWENTY - SEVEN

Jezebel ~ I'm Coming to You as a Woman Who Chose the Wrong Throne
When power turns poisonous to the soul. (1 Kings 16:31–33; 18–21; 2 Kings 9:30–37)

"I'm coming to you as a woman who misused power and paid the price."

I'm coming to you as a woman who was a queen, married to King Ahab of Israel, and I had influence that could shape the nation. But instead of using my position to honor God, I used it to promote Baal and Asherah, false gods.

I wasn't content with just having a voice in the palace. I wanted control. When the prophets of God stood in my way, I threatened their lives. When a man named Naboth refused to give Ahab his vineyard, I arranged for false accusations to have him killed. On the outside, I looked like I was winning. But, my victories were built on pride, manipulation, and rebellion; and God does not overlook those things forever.

Here's the truth I didn't want to face: Influence without submission to God is dangerous.
I thought I was untouchable. I thought I could control outcomes. But when you fight against God's order, you're setting yourself up for a fall you can't avoid. The prophet Elijah confronted me, and God's judgment was declared over my life. It didn't happen overnight but it came. My end was brutal, a fulfillment of the very prophecy I ignored. My name became a warning for generations after me.

I'm Just Coming to You as a Woman

Who knows what it's like to chase power and control so hard that you lose yourself and your life in the process. Your influence can build the kingdom of God or try to fight against it but only one choice leads to life.

Ambition without submission to God will be your undoing. Choose the throne of His presence over the seat of your own power.

What I Want You to Know

Influence is a gift but it must be surrendered to God. Pride blinds you to danger until it's too late. You can't manipulate your way into God's blessing.

Hold On To This

"Pride goes before destruction, a haughty spirit before a fall." (Proverbs 16:18). *"There is a way that seems right to a man, but its end is the way of death."* (Proverbs 14:12). *"Humble yourselves before the Lord, and He will lift you up."* (James 4:10)

I'm coming to you as a woman to tell you to never let the hunger for power or control take you so far that you forget who's really in charge.

CHAPTER TWENTY - EIGHT

Huldah ~ I'm Coming to You as a Woman Who Spoke God's Word
Courage to declare truth in a time of compromise. (2 Kings 22:14–20; 2 Chronicles 34:22–28)

"I'm coming to you as a woman who opened her mouth for God even when the message was hard."

I'm coming to you as a woman who lived in Jerusalem during the reign of King Josiah, a time when God's people had strayed far from His Word. The temple had been neglected, the Law forgotten. One day, the high priest Hilkiah found the Book of the Law while repairing the temple. When it was read to the king, his heart broke. He wanted to know if what was written was truly from God and what it meant for us. They could have gone to any prophet in the land, but they came to me.

When the officials arrived, I listened for the voice of the Lord. And He spoke.
The message wasn't light. God said judgment was coming because the people had forsaken Him and worshiped idols. But to King Josiah, because his heart was tender and he humbled himself, God promised mercy in his lifetime.

Delivering a hard word isn't easy. It would have been simpler to tell them what they wanted to hear. But when you speak for God, you don't edit His truth to make it comfortable. I wasn't a palace insider. I wasn't part of the priestly hierarchy. I was a woman with a prophetic ear and that was enough for God to use me to bring His Word to the highest authority in the land.

I'm Just Coming to You as a Woman

who knows the weight of speaking up when it would be easier to stay quiet. You may not stand before kings, but there will be moments when God asks you to say what others are afraid to speak. In those moments, be bold.

What I Want You to Know

God can use your voice to bring truth and clarity in a confused world. Courage is choosing obedience to God over the approval of people. Your authority comes from the One who sent you, not your title, your position, or your popularity.

Hold On To This

"She speaks with wisdom, and faithful instruction is on her tongue." (Proverbs 31:26). *"Do not be afraid of them, for I am with you and will rescue you, declares the Lord."* (Jeremiah 1:8). *"We must obey God rather than human beings!"* (Acts 5:29)

I'm coming to you as a woman to tell you that when God gives you a word, speak it with boldness and love, and trust Him with the results.

CHAPTER TWENTY-NINE

Daughters of Job ~ We're Coming to You as Women of Beauty After Ashes
God can restore more than you ever lost. (Job 42:13–15)

"We're coming to you as women who were born into beauty after ashes."

We are coming to you as women. We are Jemimah, Keziah, and Keren-Happuch; the daughters of Job.
Our father's story is well known: the man who lost everything; his children, his wealth, his health and yet refused to curse God. But what's often overlooked is how God restored him… and how we became part of that testimony.

We weren't the children who were lost. We were the children born after the trial.
By the time we arrived, our father had seen grief up close. He had wrestled with questions, sat in silence, and endured the counsel of friends who didn't understand. But he had also seen the goodness of God break through.

Our birth was more than a family expansion, we were living proof that the story wasn't over.

In our culture, daughters didn't usually get the spotlight in genealogies. But Scripture says we were the most beautiful women in all the land. Our names weren't just pretty sounds, they carried meaning:

- **Jemimah** — "dove," a symbol of peace after chaos.
- **Keziah** — "a spice" a fragrance of delight after bitterness.
- **Keren-Happuch** — "horn of eye-shadow," a sign of outward beauty and adornment, representing joy and restoration.

In our day, daughters didn't normally receive an inheritance when sons were present. But our father gave us an equal share alongside our brothers.

It was as if God Himself was showing that in His restoration, there's no shortage, everyone gets to partake in the overflow.

We're Just Coming to You as Women

who represent the after-story, the part of your life where God proves that loss is not the end. We are the joy born out of mourning, the beauty that follows ashes, the blessing that shows your latter can be greater than your former.

What We Want You to Know

God's restoration doesn't just replace what was lost, it exceeds it. You can be a sign to others that the storm does end. In God's kingdom, there's enough inheritance for everyone.

Hold On To This

"The Lord blessed the latter part of Job's life more than the former part." (Job 42:12). *"He will give them beauty for ashes, the oil of joy for mourning, and the garment of praise for the spirit of heaviness."* (Isaiah 61:3). *"Those who sow with tears will reap with songs of joy."* (Psalm 126:5)

We're coming to you as women to remind you that God can make your ending far more beautiful than your beginning. Your after-story is worth waiting for.

CHAPTER THIRTY

Isaiah's Wife ~ I'm Coming to You as a Mother of a Sign
Our family became part of God's prophetic story.

"I'm coming to you as a woman who carried both a child and a prophecy."

I'm coming to you as a woman, a wife, to a well known man. I am called "the prophetess" not because I was married to Isaiah the prophet, but because I too carried the voice of God.
I lived in a home where every word, every act, every decision was under the weight of God's message to His people. Together Isaiah and I named our son Maher-Shalal-Hash-Baz as a living prophecy to the nation.

When the Lord told Isaiah to write a name on a scroll, *Maher-Shalal-Hash-Baz*, it was strange enough. But then He said I would bear a son, and that this would be his name.

That name meant "Quick to the plunder, swift to the spoil."
It wasn't a cute family name or something easy to explain at the market. It was a prophecy in itself, a warning to the nation that judgment and invasion were coming quickly.

My pregnancy was not just personal, it was prophetic. Every time I felt that child move inside me, I knew the message was moving closer to fulfillment.

Living with a prophetic calling means living with tension.
We spoke words people didn't always want to hear. We carried messages that were sometimes heavy, even for our own hearts. But we also knew that obedience was more important than approval.

I had to agree with God, even when I didn't understand all the details. I had to carry the weight of His Word alongside the weight of my child.

I'm Just Coming to You as a Woman

who knows the cost of saying "yes" when your life becomes part of God's message. Friends, sometimes your life, and your children, will be God's message to the world. Walk it out faithfully.

Sometimes your calling won't just be in your mouth, it will be in your very life, your family, your story. And people will read it whether they want to or not.

What I Want You to Know

Agreeing with God may set you apart, but it will also anchor you. Sometimes your obedience is the message before you say a word. You can partner with God in ways that affect generations.

Hold On To This

"I went to the prophetess, and she conceived and gave birth to a son. And the Lord said to me, 'Name him Maher-Shalal-Hash-Baz.'" (Isaiah 8:3). *"Can two walk together, except they be agreed?"* (Amos 3:3). *"The Lord gives the word; the women who proclaim it are a mighty throng."* (Psalm 68:11)

I'm coming to you as a woman to tell you that sometimes God will make your very life the prophecy. Walk in agreement, even when the message is heavy, because it will accomplish what He intends.

Part VI

Exile & Return

When God's people were scattered, women again stood in pivotal places. Some risked their lives to save nations, while others reveal the dangers of false voices and compromised faith.

CHAPTER THIRTY - ONE

Esther ~ I'm coming to you as a woman who had Courage in the Face of Fear

"Before you're seen, you have to be prepared." (Book of Esther)

"I'm coming to you as a woman who had to risk it all for the sake of others."

I'm coming to you as a woman who didn't ask to be queen. Honestly, I was just a girl being raised by my cousin Mordecai after my parents died. Then came the beauty treatments, the royal court, and before I knew it I was wearing a crown in a palace far from everything familiar.

It looked glamorous on the outside, but inside I often felt out of place. No one knew my true identity. I was living with a secret that could cost me everything.

When Haman's plan to destroy my people came to light, fear gripped me. Mordecai's message still echoes in my heart:
"Who knows whether you have come to the kingdom for such a time as this?" (Esther 4:14)

There comes a moment when you realize God placed you exactly where you are not by accident, not for comfort, but for purpose.

I didn't rush in with a plan. I told my people, *"Go, gather all the Jews… fast for me. Do not eat or drink for three days, night or day. I and my attendants will fast as you do."* (Esther 4:16)

I needed heaven's help before I opened my mouth. Because here's the truth, going to the king without being summoned could have meant my death.

On the third day, I put on my royal robes and walked toward the throne room, my heart pounding. I didn't know if I'd live to see the next sunrise. But the king extended his golden scepter and my life was spared.

From there, God gave me wisdom to speak at the right time, in the right way. The enemy's plan was overturned, and my people were saved.

I'm Coming to You as a Woman

who knows what it's like to be afraid, to question your own strength, and to wonder if you're the right one for the assignment. I'm coming to you as a woman who learned that courage isn't the absence of fear, it's moving forward in spite of it.

What I Want You to Know

You are where you are on purpose, even if it doesn't look like it. God can use your position no matter how unlikely to protect and bless others. Prayer and fasting are not last resorts; they are first responses. Courage often comes in the walking, not in the waiting for fear to disappear.

Hold On To This

"Who knows whether you have come to the kingdom for such a time as this?" (Esther 4:14). "When I am afraid, I put my trust in You." (Psalm 56:3). "Be strong and courageous. Do not be afraid; do not be discouraged, for the Lord your God will be with you wherever you go." (Joshua 1:9)

I'm just coming to you as a woman to tell you that your voice, your courage, and your obedience could save a generation. Don't sit this one out.

CHAPTER THIRTY - TWO

Noadiah ~ I'm Coming to You as a Woman Who Warns
The cost of false prophecy and leading astray. (Nehemiah 6:14)

"I'm coming to you as a woman who misused her voice, and it didn't end well."

I'm coming to you as a woman who is often known as a false prophet because I used my voice to lead astray. My name is Noadiah, and yes, I was a prophetess. That means I had the ear of the people. My words could stir hearts, shift moods, and sway decisions. But instead of aligning with the truth of God, I let myself be driven by fear, pride, and the agendas of men.

When Nehemiah came to rebuild the wall of Jerusalem, it should have been a time of unity and restoration. But I joined those who opposed him. I spoke words meant to intimidate, to discourage, to stall the work. Why? Because deep down, I didn't want to lose the influence I had.

Friend, it's sobering how quickly the desire to protect your position can turn you into an enemy of God's mission.

Nehemiah prayed against me by name. That's how serious my opposition was. My story isn't one of repentance or redemption. Scripture simply records my name as a warning.

I'm Just Coming to You as a Woman

who learned that gifting without obedience is dangerous. You can speak under the banner of "ministry" and still work against the very thing God is doing.

What I Want You to Know

Your voice carries weight so use it to build, not tear down. Position means nothing if your heart is far from God. Just because someone is "spiritual" doesn't mean they're aligned with His Spirit.

Hold On To This

"Do not put out the Spirit's fire; do not treat prophecies with contempt. Test everything. Hold on to what is good." (1 Thessalonians 5:19-21). *"By their fruit you will recognize them."* (Matthew 7:16). *"The fear of the Lord is the beginning of wisdom, and knowledge of the Holy One is understanding."* (Proverbs 9:10)

I'm coming to you as a woman to tell you not to let pride or fear pull you out of alignment with God. Your influence is a gift; use it to serve His purpose, not your own.

CHAPTER THIRTY - THREE

Proverbs 31 Woman ~ I'm Coming to You as a Woman of Strength
Living a life worth more than rubies. (Proverbs 31:10–31)

"I'm coming to you as a woman who knows that being Proverbs 31 isn't about perfection it's about purpose."

I'm coming to you as a Proverbs 31 woman. Let's get real, sometimes when people talk about the Proverbs 31 woman, it sounds like a checklist of impossible standards.
Wake up before sunrise? Check.
Cook every meal from scratch? Check.
Manage a business, serve the poor, and still look flawless? Check, check, check.

But, that's not the heart of this woman.

The Proverbs 31 woman isn't a superhero. She's a woman who loves God and lives intentionally. She works hard, yes. She cares for her family, yes. But she also trusts God to lead her steps.

She's not worried about being perfect, she's focused on being faithful. She's not defined by how much she gets done but by who she is in God's eyes.

I'm Just Coming to You as a Woman

who has walked through days of doubt, tiredness, and feeling not enough and found that Proverbs 31 is a *calling*, not a *burden*.

What I Want You to Know

You don't have to do it all, you just have to do your part with love. Strength and dignity come from trusting God, not from striving harder. Your worth isn't measured by your productivity, but by your purpose.

Hold On To This

"**10** Who can find a virtuous woman? for her price is far above rubies. **11** The heart of her husband doth safely trust in her, so that he shall have no need of spoil. **12** She will do him good and not evil all the days of her life. **13** She seeketh wool, and flax, and worketh willingly with her hands. **14** She is like the merchants' ships; she bringeth her food from afar. **15** She riseth also while it is yet night, and giveth meat to her household, and a portion to her maidens. **16** She considereth a field, and buyeth it: with the fruit of her hands she planteth a vineyard. **17** She girdeth her loins with strength, and strengtheneth her arms. **18** She perceiveth that her merchandise is good: her candle goeth not out by night. **19** She layeth her hands to the spindle, and her hands hold the distaff. **20** She stretcheth out her hand to the poor; yea, she reacheth forth her hands to the needy. **21** She is not afraid of the snow for her household: for all her household are clothed with scarlet. **22** She maketh herself coverings of tapestry; her clothing is silk and purple. **23** Her husband is known in the gates, when he sitteth among the elders of the land. **24** She maketh fine linen, and selleth it; and delivereth girdles unto the merchant. **25** Strength and honour are her clothing; and she shall rejoice in time to come. **26** She openeth her mouth with wisdom; and in her tongue is the law of kindness. **27** She looketh well to the ways of her household, and eateth not the bread of idleness. **28** Her children arise up, and call her blessed; her husband also, and he praiseth her. **29** Many daughters have done virtuously, but thou excellest them all. **30** Favour is deceitful, and beauty is vain: but a woman that feareth the Lord, she shall be praised. **31** Give her of the fruit of her hands; and let her own works praise her in the gates. (Proverbs 31:10-31)

I'm coming to you as a woman to tell you not to let the idea of 'perfect' steal your joy. Be faithful in your purpose and watch God use you in powerful ways.

Part VII

The Coming of Christ

New Testament

After centuries of silence, women became the first to carry the promises of the Messiah. Through faith, obedience, and worship, they opened the way for God's greatest gift.

CHAPTER THIRTY - FOUR

Elizabeth ~ I'm Coming to You as a Woman Who Carried Promise
Faith in God's timing brought life to my womb. (Luke 1:5–25, 39–45, 57–66)

"I'm coming to you as a woman who learned that no season is too late for God to move."

I'm coming to you as a woman who carried promise. For years, my husband Zechariah and I prayed for a child. We served God faithfully, but my womb stayed empty. As the years passed, people probably whispered that my time had run out. And honestly, some days I believed them.

I loved the Lord, but deep down I had accepted that motherhood wasn't in my story.

Then one day, the impossible happened. The angel Gabriel appeared to Zechariah while he was serving in the temple and told him we would have a son, not just any son, but one who would prepare the way for the Lord.

I was already well past the age of childbearing. But, when God writes your story, He isn't limited by your age, your circumstances, or what people think is possible.

When I became pregnant, I stayed in seclusion for five months. Not because I was ashamed, but because I was overwhelmed with awe. I needed that time to sit with the miracle, to let gratitude sink deep, to worship in private before the celebration went public.

Six months into my pregnancy, my cousin Mary came to visit. The moment she greeted me, the baby inside me leaped for joy. And I was filled with the Holy Spirit. I recognized then that the child Mary carried was the promised Messiah.

That moment taught me something important. Sometimes your miracle will recognize someone else's miracle, and both will be confirmed in God's presence.

I'm Just Coming to You as a Woman

who has waited long, prayed hard, and seen God move in ways I couldn't have imagined. No matter how delayed the promise feels, when it comes, it will be right on time.

What I Want You to Know

Delayed doesn't mean denied. God's timing is perfect. Private praise prepares you for public testimony. God's miracles often connect us to others for mutual encouragement.

Hold On To This

"This is what the Lord has done for me… He has shown His favor and taken away my disgrace among the people." (Luke 1:25). *"For no word from God will ever fail."* (Luke 1:37). *"Blessed is she who has believed that the Lord would fulfill His promises to her!"* (Luke 1:45)

I'm coming to you as a woman to tell you that you're never too old, too far gone, or too late for God to surprise you with a promise fulfilled.

CHAPTER THIRTY - FIVE

Mary, Mother of Jesus ~ I'm Coming to You as a Woman Who Said Yes

Obedience opened the door for the Savior's birth. (Luke 1:26–38; 2; John 19:25–27)

" I'm coming to you as a woman who said 'yes' when the world said 'no.'"

I'm coming to you as a woman who knows what it feels like to say yes to God while facing criticism, gossip and isolation. I was just a young woman; ordinary, living my everyday life; when an angel showed up with a message that would change everything.
"You will conceive and give birth to a son, and you are to call Him Jesus." (Luke 1:31)

I won't lie, my first thought was fear. How could this be? How would my family react? What about Joseph?
But in the middle of my questions and doubts, I made a choice: I said, *"I am the Lord's servant. May your word to me be fulfilled."* (Luke 1:38)

Saying yes to God doesn't mean the path is easy.
There were long nights wondering how I would care for this child, journeys on dusty roads, and the pain of watching Him face rejection and sacrifice.

But through it all, I held onto one truth, God's plan is always bigger than my fear, my doubts, or my circumstances.

Even when the shepherds and wise men came, even when Simeon prophesied about the sword that would pierce my soul, I trusted.
I treasured every moment, every word, every miracle; holding them close in my heart, knowing God was working through my son to change the world.

I'm Just Coming to You as a Woman

who knows what it means to face the unknown and still say yes. To carry a promise in your womb, a calling in your heart, and a hope in your soul; even when the road is rocky and the future unclear.

What I Want You to Know

Saying yes to God may bring unexpected challenges, but it also brings unparalleled blessings. Faith isn't about having all the answers; it's about trusting the One who does.
Keep your heart soft and your spirit ready. God often uses the quietest women to change the loudest places.

Hold On To This

"My soul glorifies the Lord and my spirit rejoices in God my Savior." (Luke 1:46-47). *"For nothing will be impossible with God."* (Luke 1:37). *"Blessed is she who has believed that the Lord would fulfill His promises to her!"* (Luke 1:45)

I'm coming to you as a woman to tell you to say yes when He calls, walk with courage, and trust that your obedience will write history.

CHAPTER THIRTY - SIX

Anna ~ I'm Coming to You as a Woman Who Waited in Worship
Years in prayer prepared me to see the Messiah. (Luke 2:36–38)

"I'm coming to you as a woman who learned that waiting is never wasted when your eyes are on God."

I'm coming to you as a woman dedicated to God. I was young when I married, but only seven years into our marriage, my husband died. I never remarried. Instead, I devoted the rest of my life to serving God in His temple.

For decades, I prayed. I fasted. I worshiped. Day and night. Some might have called my life empty. But I knew that when you're in God's presence, you're never without purpose.

I didn't have a timeline for the promise I was waiting for. The Scriptures spoke of the Messiah, the One who would redeem Israel, but no one knew when He would come.

Still, I stayed.
I kept my post.
I chose to trust that one day, I'd see what God had promised.

Then one day, I saw a young couple walk into the temple holding a baby boy. The moment my eyes fell on Him, I knew this was the Messiah.

I began praising God right there. My waiting had ended. I couldn't keep the news to myself, I spoke about Him to everyone who was looking for redemption.

I'm Just Coming to You as a Woman

who knows what it's like to stay faithful even when the promise feels far away. The world may not understand your dedication, but God sees it. And when the day comes, your faithfulness will meet its fulfillment. Don't waste your waiting. Worship in it. The fulfillment of God's promise will be worth every year you've spent on your knees.

What I Want You to Know

A life devoted to God is never wasted, no matter how hidden it feels. Faithfulness in the small, unseen days prepares you for the big, revealed ones. When God fulfills His promise, it will all make sense.

Hold On To This

"She never left the temple but worshiped night and day, fasting and praying." (Luke 2:37). "Let us not become weary in doing good, for at the proper time we will reap a harvest if we do not give up." (Galatians 6:9). "The Lord is good to those whose hope is in Him, to the one who seeks Him." (Lamentations 3:25)

I'm coming to you as a woman to tell you to stay faithful in your waiting. God's promises have perfect timing, and when they come, you won't be able to keep quiet about what He's done.

Part VIII

Part VIII

Women in Jesus' Ministry

Jesus honored women in ways His culture often did not. Their testimonies, tears, and worship shaped the story of the Gospel making them witnesses to His power and resurrection.

CHAPTER THIRTY - SEVEN

Samaritan Woman ~ I'm Coming to You as a Woman Who Dropped Her Jar
My shame became my testimony. (John 4:1–42)

"I'm coming to you as a woman who came thirsty for water and left overflowing with life."

I'm coming to you as a woman whose life speaks louder than her name. My name? You don't know it.
The Scriptures didn't tell you. But you know my story.
I came to Jacob's well at noon, in the heat of the day because I didn't want to see anyone. People talked about me. Whispered about me. I had been with five husbands, and the man I lived with wasn't my husband at all.

I didn't need more judgment. I just needed water.

That day, a Jewish man sat by the well. He asked me for a drink. That alone shocked me, Jews didn't talk to Samaritans, and men didn't publicly talk to women like me.

Then He said something stranger: *"If you knew the gift of God and who it is that asks you for a drink, you would have asked Him, and He would have given you living water."*

We talked about my life. He told me things he had no way of knowing. He spoke of worship not being about a mountain or a temple, but about spirit and truth. And then He said plainly: *"I, the one speaking to you, I am He."*

The Messiah. Right there at my well. Speaking to me.

I dropped my water jar, the very reason I came, and ran into town. "Come, see a man who told me everything I ever did. Could this be the Messiah?"

People listened. They came. Many believed because of my testimony, and even more after meeting Him for themselves.

I'm Just Coming to You as a Woman

who met Jesus in the middle of her shame and left changed.
You don't have to have it all together for Him to meet you.
You don't have to hide your past for Him to use you.

What I Want You to Know

Jesus will meet you right where you are, even in the heat of your hiding place. Your testimony can draw others to Christ, no matter your past. Once you've tasted living water, you'll never be satisfied with anything else.

Hold On To This

"Whoever drinks the water I give them will never thirst." (John 4:14). "Come and see what God has done." (Psalm 66:5). *"Therefore, there is now no condemnation for those who are in Christ Jesus."* (Romans 8:1)

I'm coming to you as a woman to tell you not to wait until you feel worthy to meet Jesus. Come thirsty, and let Him fill you until you overflow into the lives of others.

CHAPTER THIRTY - EIGHT

Mary Magdalene ~ I'm Coming to You as a Woman Delivered
From bondage to the first to see Him risen. (Luke 8:1–3; John 20:1–18)

"I'm coming to you as a woman who's been through the fire and found new life on the other side."

I'm coming to you as a woman who didn't have a great reputation. I wasn't always who you see in the Bible. I was a woman haunted, several demons had taken hold of me, leaving me broken, rejected, and desperate. People looked at me and saw my past, but Jesus saw my worth.

Jesus cast the demons out of me, and I followed Him faithfully. On resurrection morning, He called my name.

When He found me, He didn't push me away or condemn me. He healed me; body, mind, and soul. I became one of His closest followers, standing by Him through the hardest moments, even when others ran away.

I was the first to see Him alive after the resurrection, and the first to share the good news.
That means He trusted me with the most important message ever told.

What I Want You to Know

No matter your past, God can rewrite your story. Your scars don't disqualify you, they testify to His grace. Faithfulness isn't about perfection, but persistence.

I'm Just Coming to You as a Woman

who knows what it's like to be misunderstood, overlooked, and yet chosen. Deliverance makes you a witness. Tell what He's done for you! If God can use me, He can use you too, no matter what you've been through.

Hold On To This

"Jesus said to her, 'Mary.' She turned and said to Him in Aramaic, 'Rabboni!' (which means Teacher)." (John 20:16). *"Therefore, if anyone is in Christ, the new creation has come: The old has gone, the new is here!"* (2 Corinthians 5:17). *"My grace is sufficient for you, for my power is made perfect in weakness."* (2 Corinthians 12:9)

I'm coming to you as a woman to tell you that no matter what you've faced, you are chosen, loved, and called to rise.

CHAPTER THIRTY - NINE

Martha ~ I'm Coming to You as a Woman Who Served
Learning when to sit and when to serve. (Luke 10:38–42; John 11:1–44)

"I'm coming to you as a woman who let busyness get in the way of presence."

I'm coming to you as a woman who knows what it feels like to keep herself busy. When you hear my name, you probably think of the day Jesus came to our home.
I wanted everything to be perfect; the bread fresh, the table set just right, the house in order. Hospitality wasn't just something I did; it was part of how I showed love.

But in my desire to serve Him well, I missed the better part of the moment.

My sister Mary sat at His feet, listening to every word.
I was running back and forth in the kitchen, my mind spinning with to-do lists, my heart frustrated that she wasn't helping me.

Finally, I went to Jesus and said, *"Lord, don't You care that my sister has left me to serve alone? Tell her to help me!"* (Luke 10:40)

His answer still humbles me:
"Martha, Martha, you are worried and upset about many things, but only one thing is needed. Mary has chosen the better part, and it will not be taken away from her." (Luke 10:41-42)

It wasn't that my service was wrong, it's that my priorities were.
Jesus wasn't asking me to abandon serving; He was inviting me to first sit in His presence, to let my heart be filled before my hands got busy.

Later, when my brother Lazarus died, I ran to meet Jesus before He even reached the village. My heart still believed in His power. And I heard Him say, *"I am the resurrection and the life."* (John 11:25). In that moment, I realized the same truth Mary had learned, being close to Him mattered more than anything else.

I'm Just Coming to You as a Woman

who knows the pressure to get it all done and the guilt when you feel like you can't.
But I've learned that presence fuels purpose. You can't pour out what you haven't received.

What I Want You to Know

Don't let the urgent crowd out the important. Jesus values your attention more than your activity.
Your service will be richer when it flows from time spent with Him.

Hold On To This

"Be still, and know that I am God." (Psalm 46:10). "Come to me, all you who are weary and burdened, and I will give you rest." (Matthew 11:28). "Better is one day in your courts than a thousand elsewhere." (Psalm 84:10)

I'm coming to you as a woman to tell you that before you serve Him with your hands, sit with Him with your heart. The dishes can wait. His presence can't.

CHAPTER FORTY

Mary of Bethany ~ I'm Coming to You as a Woman Who Sat at His Feet
Choosing the Better Part (Luke 10:38–42; John 11–12)

"I'm coming to you as a woman who learned that time at His feet is never wasted."

I'm coming to you as a woman who chose the better part! I remember the day clearly, the day Jesus came to our home. Martha bustled around, working hard to prepare everything just right. She loved Him deeply, and serving was her way of showing it. Me? I sat down at His feet. I didn't care if the bread was ready or if the table was set. All I cared about was hearing His voice.

When Martha came into the room upset, asking Jesus to tell me to help her, I held my breath.
But He looked at her with love and said, *"Mary has chosen the better part, and it will not be taken away from her."* (Luke 10:42). That moment taught me this: there will always be things to do, but there won't always be this moment, this chance to sit close, to listen deeply, to be with Him.

Later, when my brother Lazarus died, I fell at Jesus' feet again, but this time in tears. Even in my grief, I knew this was where I belonged. And then there was the night before His death, when I broke open a jar of expensive perfume and anointed His feet. People called it waste. Jesus called it beautiful.

I'm Just Coming to You as a Woman

who has chosen presence over performance, devotion over distraction. The world may not understand, but the One who matters most will never overlook it.

What I Want You to Know

Sitting with Jesus is not neglect, it's priority. Your devotion will be remembered long after your duties are done. What you pour out at His feet will never be wasted.

Hold On To This

"Mary has chosen the better part, and it will not be taken away from her." (Luke 10:42). *"Better is one day in Your courts than a thousand elsewhere."* (Psalm 84:10). *"The King is enthralled by your beauty; honor Him, for He is your Lord."* (Psalm 45:11)

I'm coming to you as a woman to tell you that the best thing you can give Jesus is not your schedule, but yourself. Sit at His feet, and let His words change your life.

CHAPTER FORTY - ONE

Joanna ~ I'm Coming to You as a Woman Who Supported the Mission

My resources served the One who saved me. (Luke 8:1–3; 24:10)

"I'm coming to you as a woman who decided to put her life and resources where her faith was."

I'm coming to you as a woman who traveled with Jesus. I traveled with Jesus, using my own means to provide for Him and the disciples. Serving Him was my greatest honor.

You may have heard of me in passing, I'm Joanna, the wife of Chuza, who managed the household for King Herod.
Yes, that Herod, the one whose palace was full of politics, wealth, and whispers.

I had access to influence, privilege, and comfort. But I also had an illness that no doctor could fix. Then I met Jesus. He healed me, and in that moment, my priorities shifted forever.

I could have stayed in the palace, living out my days in quiet luxury. Instead, I joined the women who traveled with Jesus and His disciples. We weren't just spectators; we served, we supported, we stood by Him in public and in private.

Yes, that meant giving my own money to fund the ministry. But it also meant giving my time, my energy, and my reputation. Not everyone understood. Some whispered, "Why would she leave all that to follow a rabbi from Nazareth?"

I wasn't there just for the miracles. I was there for the mission. I stayed through the dusty roads, the long days, the constant crowds.
And when He was crucified, I didn't disappear. I went to the tomb with the other women. And I was among the first to hear the angels say, *"He is not here; He is risen!"*

I'm Just Coming to You as a Woman

who knows what it's like to choose Kingdom over comfort.
It's not that wealth or position are wrong; it's that they should never be your master. When you've met the One who gave you life, the only reasonable response is to give that life back to Him. Friend, your provision is a ministry. What you give sustains the work of the Kingdom.

What I Want You to Know

Your resources; money, time, influence; are tools for the Kingdom. Following Jesus will cost you something, but it's worth everything. Don't just receive from Jesus; serve alongside Him.

Hold On To This

"Joanna the wife of Chuza, the manager of Herod's household; Susanna; and many others. These women were helping to support them out of their own means." (Luke 8:3). *"Where your treasure is, there your heart will be also."* (Matthew 6:21). *"Each of you should use whatever gift you have received to serve others…"* (1 Peter 4:10)

I'm coming to you as a woman to tell you to invest your life in something eternal. You'll never regret what you give to the One who gave everything for you.

CHAPTER FORTY - TWO

Woman with the Issue of Blood ~ I'm Coming to You as a Woman Who Touched the Hem

One reach changed everything. (Mark 5:25–34; Luke 8:43–48)

"I'm coming to you as a woman who was tired of suffering in silence and dared to reach for healing."

I'm coming to you as a woman who was made whole. For twelve years, I bled.
Twelve years of weakness. Twelve years of shame. Twelve years of spending everything I had on doctors who couldn't help me.

I was unclean by the law. That meant I couldn't go into the temple. I couldn't touch people. People couldn't touch me. I was alive, but cut off. Then I heard about Jesus. I heard He opened blind eyes, healed lepers, made the lame walk. I thought, *If He can do that for them, He can heal me too.*

But I was too ashamed to call out to Him in public. I didn't want to explain my condition again. So I decided, *If I can just touch His clothes, I will be healed.* I pressed through the crowd. Every step took effort. Every jolt of my body made the bleeding worse. But I kept moving until my fingers brushed the hem of His garment.

Immediately, I felt it, the flow stopped. Strength filled my body. Jesus stopped too. He turned and asked, *"Who touched Me?"* Trembling, I fell at His feet and told Him everything. And He said, *"Daughter, your faith has healed you. Go in peace and be freed from your suffering."*

I'm Just Coming to You as a Woman

Who knows what it's like to be desperate, to hide your pain, and to feel like healing is for everyone else but you. Jesus sees you. He welcomes your reach.

What I Want You to Know

Don't let shame keep you from coming to Jesus. Sometimes healing requires pressing past the crowd. Faith may start as a whisper but it can end in a miracle.

Hold On To This

"If I just touch His clothes, I will be healed." (Mark 5:28). *"Daughter, your faith has healed you. Go in peace."* (Luke 8:48). *"Come to Me, all you who are weary and burdened, and I will give you rest."* (Matthew 11:28)

I'm coming to you as a woman to tell you that you may have been carrying your pain for years, but one reach toward Jesus can change your story forever.

Part IX

The Early Church

After Christ's ascension, women did not fade into silence. They led house churches, financed missions, prophesied, and even carried the very letters of Paul, proving God's call includes them too.

CHAPTER FORTY-THREE

Dorcas (Tabitha) ~ I'm Coming to You as a Woman Who Clothed the Needy
My hands became my ministry. (Acts 9:36–42)

"I'm coming to you as a woman whose hands preached the Gospel before her mouth ever did."

I'm coming to you as a woman named Tabitha. Others called me Dorcas. Either way, my name meant "gazelle", graceful, quick to move. And that's how I lived my life: quick to move toward those in need.

I didn't preach sermons or stand in the synagogue teaching. My ministry was in my needle and thread. I made garments for widows, the ones often overlooked and left out. I didn't just hand them clothes; I wrapped them in dignity.

I never thought my work was grand enough to be remembered. I simply saw needs and met them. But love is loud, even when the actions are quiet. Word spread that I cared for people when no one else did. My home was filled with fabric, laughter, and the occasional tear as women shared their stories while I sewed.

Then one day, I got sick. And I died.
The community I had served felt the loss deeply. The widows I'd clothed gathered around, weeping, showing the garments I had made for them.

They sent for Peter, one of the apostles. He came, prayed, and told me to get up. And by the power of God, I did.

After that, my story wasn't just about kindness anymore. It was about the God who sees service done in secret and honors it in ways you can't imagine. I learned that even the smallest acts of love can ripple into eternity and sometimes, God will write a resurrection into your story to make sure it keeps going.

I'm Just Coming to You as a Woman

who knows that ministry isn't always on a stage. Sometimes it's in your kitchen, your workshop, or your everyday tasks. Your faithfulness in the little can leave a legacy that others will fight to keep alive. Your work may seem simple, but in God's hands, it's sacred.

What I Want You to Know

Ministry is not about visibility; it's about impact. God sees every act of kindness, even the ones no one else notices. Love can be a language louder than words.

Hold On To This

"In Joppa there was a disciple named Tabitha… who was always doing good and helping the poor." (Acts 9:36). *"Let us not become weary in doing good…"* (Galatians 6:9). *"Whatever you do, work at it with all your heart, as working for the Lord…"* (Colossians 3:23)

I'm coming to you as a woman to tell you to keep loving, keep serving, and keep giving. You have no idea how far the thread you're weaving will reach.

CHAPTER FORTY - FOUR

Daughters of Philip ~ We're Coming to You as Women Who Speak Truth
Raising the next generation of bold voices. (Acts 21:8–9)

"We're coming to you as women who grew up in the presence of the Gospel and chose to carry it forward."

"**We are coming to you as women** who are the four daughters of Philip the evangelist.
Our father was one of the seven chosen to serve in the early church, a man full of the Spirit and wisdom. He preached in Samaria, baptized the Ethiopian eunuch, and opened the door for the Gospel to cross cultural lines.

We grew up hearing the Good News not just in the streets, but around our own table.

All four of us walked in the gift of prophecy.
That meant speaking under the inspiration of the Holy Spirit; sometimes encouragement, sometimes correction, sometimes a word of direction.

We didn't need a public title to make an eternal impact. We just needed obedience. Our voices weren't for entertainment or self-promotion, they were instruments for the Kingdom.

Our father's life taught us that the Gospel is worth going wherever God sends you.
But our home life taught us that the Gospel starts where you live. We saw hospitality, prayer, and boldness modeled daily. And when it was our turn to speak, we were ready.

We're Just Coming to You as Women

who know the privilege and responsibility of using your voice for God. You may feel small or overlooked, but when the Spirit speaks through you, Heaven takes notice.

What We Want You to Know

Your spiritual gifts are meant to be used, not hidden. Your home can be a training ground for Kingdom work. Your voice matters in the plan of God.

Hold On To This

"We entered the house of Philip the evangelist… He had four unmarried daughters who prophesied." (Acts 21:8-9). *"I will pour out my Spirit on all people. Your sons and daughters will prophesy…"* (Acts 2:17). *"Each of you should use whatever gift you have received to serve others…"* (1 Peter 4:10)

We're coming to you as women to tell you to open your mouth when God gives you something to say. You never know whose life will change because you chose to speak.

CHAPTER FORTY-FIVE

Phoebe ~ I'm Coming to You as a Woman Trusted with the Word
Faithfully carrying God's message to His people. (Romans 16:1–2)

"I'm coming to you as a woman who carried the Word, not just in scrolls, but in my life."

I'm coming to you as a woman who loves to serve. My name is Phoebe. Paul called me a servant, in the Greek, a *diakonos* (Deacon) of the church in Cenchreae. He entrusted me with something precious: the letter you now call Romans. I didn't just deliver words. I carried a message from God's heart to His people. I wasn't just a messenger. I was a benefactor, a patron for many, including Paul himself. My resources, my home, my hands were open to the work of the Kingdom. Serving God's people wasn't a side task for me. It was my life.

I'm Just Coming to You as a Woman

who knows that carrying God's Word is a calling, whether in your hands, your mouth, or your actions. Your influence is not small when your obedience is big.

What I Want You to Know

Service in the Kingdom is leadership in the Kingdom. God can trust you with much when you're faithful with little. Your generosity can advance the gospel farther than you imagine.

Hold On To This

"I commend to you our sister Phoebe, a servant of the church in Cenchreae." (Romans 16:1). *"Well done, good and faithful servant."* (Matthew 25:23). *"Each of you should use whatever gift you have received to serve others."* (1 Peter 4:10)

I'm coming to you as a woman to tell you not to underestimate the power of being faithful with the assignment God puts in your hands. It can change nations.

CHAPTER FORTY - SIX

Priscilla ~ I'm Coming to You as a Woman Who Taught Truth
Shaping lives from my home table. (Acts 18:1–3, 18–28; Romans 16:3–5)

"I'm coming to you as a woman who opened her home and her mouth for the gospel."

I'm coming to you as a woman who taught the truth. My name is Priscilla.
I worked leather and canvas alongside my husband, Aquila. We made tents but our true work was building the Church.

One day, a man named Apollos came to Ephesus. He was gifted in speaking and knew the Scriptures but his understanding was incomplete.
Aquila and I invited him into our home and explained the way of God more accurately. We didn't embarrass him; we empowered him. That's what Kingdom teaching does.

Sometimes my name was listed before my husband's in Scripture, not because I was more important, but because God's work through me was visible and significant. We were partners in the gospel, equal in the labor, united in purpose.

I'm Just Coming to You as a Woman

who knows that teaching the truth is just as important as preaching it. You don't have to stand on a stage to shape nations, you can shape them from your table.

What I Want You to Know

Teaching is discipleship, and discipleship changes the world. Ministry in marriage is partnership, not competition. Hospitality opens hearts for truth to take root.

Hold On To This

"Priscilla and Aquila… explained to him the way of God more adequately." (Acts 18:26). *"Let the message of Christ dwell among you richly as you teach and admonish one another."* (Colossians 3:16). *"Go and make disciples of all nations."* (Matthew 28:19)

I'm coming to you as a woman to tell you to open your door, open your Bible, and open your mouth. God can use all three to expand His Kingdom.

CHAPTER FORTY - SEVEN

Junia ~ I'm Coming to You as a Woman Known Among the Apostles
God writes women's names in His story. (Romans 16:7)

"I'm coming to you as a woman whose name still stands as a reminder that women have always been part of building the Kingdom."

I'm coming to you as a woman who didn't let my gender get in the way of my purpose. My name is Junia.

You may not hear my name preached often, but it's there in Paul's letter to the Romans: *"Greet Andronicus and Junia, my fellow Jews who have been in prison with me. They are outstanding among the apostles, and they were in Christ before I was."* (Romans 16:7)

That's me.
 A woman, a believer before Paul, called "outstanding among the apostles."

I served alongside my husband, Andronicus. We carried the gospel, we planted and strengthened churches, and yes we suffered for it.
Prison cells weren't unfamiliar. Hardship didn't surprise us. But neither did miracles. We lived for the Name that saved us.

For centuries, some tried to change my name in the Scriptures to make it sound masculine. They couldn't believe a woman could be an apostle. But the truth remains: I was there. I did the work. I bore the scars. My life says what my name doesn't have to shout: the gospel is for all, and the work of ministry is for all whom God calls.

I'm Just Coming to You as a Woman

who wants you to remember: titles don't limit you, and gender doesn't disqualify you.
If God calls you, He equips you and the fruit of your life will speak louder than anyone's opinion.

What I Want You to Know

Don't shrink your calling to fit someone else's comfort zone. The ministry isn't safe, but it's worth every cost. God's recognition of your work matters more than man's approval.

Hold On To This

"Greet Andronicus and Junia… outstanding among the apostles." (Romans 16:7). *"The Lord gives the word; the women who proclaim the good news are a great host."* (Psalm 68:11). *"We must obey God rather than human beings!"* (Acts 5:29)

I'm coming to you as a woman to tell you to never believe the lie that you're "less than" in the Kingdom. God writes women's names in His story, and no man can erase them.

Closing

Be Made Whole

An invitation to step into healing, calling, and fullness in Christ.

CHAPTER FORTY - EIGHT

Woman, Be Made Whole
An invitation to step into healing, calling, and fullness in Christ.

"I'm coming to you as a woman not just to remind you of who you've been, but to declare who you are becoming."

We've walked through stories of women like Sarah, Hagar, Rebekah, Leah, Rachel, Miriam, Deborah, Ruth, Hannah, Esther, Mary, Mary Magdalene, and even the Proverbs 31 woman. Each of their lives was messy, miraculous, painful, and full of purpose.

But here's the truth I want to leave you with:
You are not defined by your past, your pain, or your mistakes.
You are defined by God's love for you; a love that heals, restores, and makes you whole.

No matter what brokenness you carry; rejection, fear, envy, disappointment; God wants you whole.
Wholeness isn't about perfection; it's about being fully embraced by God's grace, walking in freedom, and living your destiny without shame.

It's time to lay down every weight that's holding you back.
It's time to stop hiding, stop running, and stop trying to fix it all on your own.
God is calling you to come as you are; tired, hurting, hopeful, and ready for more.

I pray you hear the whisper behind every story in this book:

May your heart find peace where there was pain.
May your faith rise where there was doubt.
May your joy shine where there was sorrow.
And may your life overflow with the fullness of God's love.

Remember This

"Come to me, all who are weary and burdened, and I will give you rest." (Matthew 11:28). *"He heals the brokenhearted and binds up their wounds."* (Psalm 147:3). *"And the God of all grace… will restore, confirm, strengthen, and establish you."* (1 Peter 5:10)

I'm coming to you as a woman; not to fix you, but to remind you that in God's eyes, you are already whole. Now, walk in that truth and watch your life transform.

Father,

I lift up my friend right now, the one who has turned these pages with an open heart, hungry for Your voice. Thank You that they are not here by accident. Thank You that from the moment they were formed in their mother's womb, You saw them, You knew them, and You called them by name.

Lord, heal the parts of their story that still feel broken. Pour Your oil on every wound, the visible ones and the hidden ones. Restore what was stolen, redeem what was lost, and breathe new life into what they thought was too far gone.

I speak courage into their spirit now, courage to trust You like Sarah, to worship like Miriam, to stand like Deborah, to press through like the woman who touched the hem, and to testify like the Samaritan woman. Let them be a carrier of Your Word like Phoebe, a teacher of truth like Priscilla, and a living witness of grace like Mary Magdalene.

Father, let them leave this moment knowing that they are not forgotten, they are not disqualified, and they are not alone.
Remind them that they are loved, chosen, and sent.

Now, in the name of Jesus, I declare over them:
Be made whole.
Be made strong.
Be made ready.

Amen.

Epilogue

The Women Still Speak

A Prophetic Charge for Today

I Came to you as a woman

Friend, as you close this book and step back into your life, I want you to carry this blessing with you like a shield and a song.

May you walk boldly into every room, knowing you are chosen, called, and equipped by God.
May your steps be sure, your heart fearless, and your spirit unshakable.

May you shine brightly not because you have to be perfect, but because God's light is alive in you. May your voice speak truth, your hands build, and your love heal wherever you go.

I declare and decree that this is a season of divine destiny, connection and clarity and I prophesy that every door meant for you be opened in Jesus name.

I prophesy that every door meant for you in this season shall swing open; doors of opportunity, doors of breakthrough, doors of divine partnership. *"Behold, I have set before you an open door, which no man can shut"* (Revelation 3:8).

This is a time of divine connections. The Lord is aligning you with the right voices, the right people, the right places. Just as Jonathan's soul was knit to David's (1 Samuel 18:1), so shall the Lord send covenant relationships that will propel you into purpose. Every counterfeit connection is being cut off, and every kingdom connection is being released, in Jesus Name.

This is a season of clarity. The fog is lifting, the noise is silenced, and the whisper of the Spirit is being made clear in your ear. *"My sheep listen to my voice; I know them, and they follow me"* (John 10:27). You will not be deceived, distracted, or delayed.

I decree that every closed door that was not meant for you will stay closed, for protection, not rejection. And every God ordained door will be undeniable. In Jesus name.

Remember, that you have purpose, power, and promise.
And no matter what comes, you never walk alone.

Go with God's peace, carry His joy, and live your life as the individual that God has created you to be.

"I'm coming to you as a woman"

not just to remind you of who you've been, but to *invite* you into who you are becoming. This is your moment. Don't let these pages be the end of your journey but let them be the spark that ignites a new chapter in your life.

You are not just a reader, you are on the move, you have a voice, and you have destiny.

So go ahead, rise up. Walk out boldly. Shine your light. The world is waiting.

"I'm coming to you as a woman and I believe in the incredible individual that God made you to be".

www.ingramcontent.com/pod-product-compliance
Lightning Source LLC
Chambersburg PA
CBHW060032180426
43196CB00045B/2621